Seeing Afresh

John + Ruth,

Thank you for so
clearly living out
+ showing us what
it means to walk
with Jesus.

With our love,

David

Seeing Afresh

Learning from Fresh Expressions of Church

David McCarthy

SAINT ANDREW PRESS

First published in 2019 by
SAINT ANDREW PRESS
121 George Street
Edinburgh EH2 4YN

ISBN 978 0 7152 0977 6

British Library Cataloguing in Publication Data

A catalogue record for this book is available from the British Library.

It is the publisher's policy to only use papers that are natural and
recyclable and that have been manufactured from timber grown
in renewable, properly managed forests. All of the manufacturing
processes of the papers are expected to conform to the environmental
regulations of the country of origin.

Typeset by Manila Typesetting Company

Printed and bound in the United Kingdom by
CPI Group (UK) Ltd

Contents

To Margaret, who so naturally lives out what I, too often, just think about.

Acknowledgements

'You wanted advice, you said. I never give advice. Never. But, I might just say this. Always search for truth.'[1]

So said the Doctor in one of his early adventures, and in my life many people have pointed me in the same direction and helped me along the way. The putting together of this book has been no exception and so I would like to say 'thank you' to many people, but can only mention a few . . .

To the churches and teams of which I've been a part and in particular to Lesley, who with vision, wisdom and grace leads the Church Without Walls team; thank you for your encouragement, insightfulness and sense of humour.

To the church communities who agreed to be interviewed and to the individuals who contributed articles; you have experienced much and have much to share. Thank you for allowing us to glimpse your stories.

To Guy and Ken, who read parts of the first draft, and to Margaret who worked through the early drafts with me; thank you for your perceptiveness, questions and enthusiasm. A particular thank you to Claire, who has been incredible: with clarity, acumen, empathy and an eagle eye for detail she has been involved in every stage.

To Saint Andrew Press, thank you for seeing the potential in this project and to Christine, thank you for guiding us through the process.

Margaret, to whom this book is dedicated, thank you for your love and support and finally, the Doctor's advice was to search for truth; thank you to the Truth who has found us.

Note

1 Terry Nation, 'The Daleks' (broadcast BBC, 21 December 1963 to 1 February 1964). Quoted in Scott, Cavan and Wright, Mark, *Wit, Wisdom and Timey-Wimey Stuff* (London: BBC Books, 2014), p. 310.

Foreword

by Rachel Jordan-Wolf

This book is a pleasure to read, David writes creatively so that he almost paints the story of Fresh Expressions in Scotland. It is a celebration of all that God has done breathing new life into his Church. It is a joy for me to read as I have visited Scotland several times to encourage this burgeoning movement. Here in these pages is a vivid description of just some of the fruit of what has been sown by so many.

David starts his book with an excellent description and basic introduction of fresh expressions, building a foundation for this movement and looking at some of the big questions behind it. He discusses the nature of church, reflects on the importance of listening to the context, and explains how fresh expressions are created, not just alongside those currently outside church, but with them. He reminds us of the importance of prayer and hospitality, and weaves throughout Chapter 1 an emphasis on relationship, God's intrinsic nature in the trinity, His invitation to us, through Jesus, to be in relationship with him and others – the foundation of church.

David brilliantly goes on to focus on our motivation behind fresh expressions – love of the other. The same drive in God – love of the other – that he gives to us. He highlights the head-on clash between love of the other and our current individualistic culture that has penetrated our churches. This is a timely calling to every Christian to see clearly the radical counter-cultural call of God to love others, which is the basis for any community following Jesus, and to examine ourselves to see how much the prevailing privatised individualistic nature of our current culture has impacted on us and our churches. His examination of how the privatisation of culture has led to the privatisation and 'personalisation' of faith, which has resulted in our inability to do mission and to talk about Jesus and simply share him with others, is a clear warning to the whole church. He shows how in fresh expressions Christians are rediscovering passion for others and community that breaks down privatised faith and creates passionate Christians who bear the image of Jesus and share him with others. He celebrates the pioneers, a gift to the whole church, to refresh us in our mission.

Another important point that I found particularly helpful in our current context is how David draws out both the importance of creating a community with people not for them, and yet how this co-building community doesn't mean that discernment for direction and setting the culture is shared equally. He uses Jesus as an example of incarnation bringing hope and challenge to the human context – Jesus clearly challenges the culture of the day and sets a clear new direction for his new community of hope.

The wonderful stories that illustrate this book are imaginative, but frequently celebrate the brave yet simple: simple steps of faith by normal pioneers in their own contexts to reach others, using messy church, cafes, alpha; inspiration that helps many to see that reaching out is possible for the many not just the few. This is not to diminish the incredible achievement of each of these, but rather to highlight that this is possible in so many more contexts.

David goes on to help with practical subjects in Part 3, looking at releasing vision, facing fear, recognising the tension between vision and reality, and importantly focusing on leadership. What sort of leaders we need for the missionary task and how in Scotland their 'going for growth' team has worked to model the principles of listening and hospitality in the way they have developed fresh expressions and leaders. He himself models community in opening the book up so that other key leaders in the FX movement in Scotland can share their wisdom in these areas. As these writers join their voices to the chorus the inescapable theme of the book emerges again – the centrality of relationship in mission.

David then leads us to the crucial debate of the day: discipleship. He talks of discipleship that is relational, communal and based in the everyday, where we are all apprentices. He stresses the mutuality of discipleship in fresh expressions, for leaders and all new community members alike, all following one master – Jesus. He discusses the need to be clearly Christian as we form new communities so that we have integrity, and how it is a constant tension to choose what to affirm and what to challenge as the new community forms in the new place. I particularly like the final thought which is a call to prayer as we walk in the complexity of the new mission field in which we find ourselves.

In Chapter 8 David is joined by other voices as we are led into the depth of learning that the team has gained from some fresh expressions. Primarily that deepening discipleship and nurturing faith has led to culture change, new life and growth. This chapter also grapples with the realities of parish life, confusion from different visions of how the new will impact the old, the weariness of many in church leadership, the frequent lack of capacity for leaders to begin the new while maintaining the old which leads to the importance of prayer. It looks at how a core learning community worked to overcome the obstacles and enable the birth of fresh expressions in the parish context. It should also be mentioned that the book examines the visionary Sanctuary First, a worshipping community that meets online. In all these examples it is impossible to escape the interdependence of discipleship and mission, as community is formed, deeper relationships created, and people grow together following Jesus.

In Part 4 David lifts us off the page and encourages us to reach for the stars even while dealing with the realities of parish life and the challenge ahead for us all. He holds up a mirror in front of our faces to see our own limited vision of the world and challenges all readers to be risk takers for the kingdom.

This book is a fantastic summary of the start of the ongoing movement of Fresh Expressions in Scotland. More than that it upholds a vision and a call to go on an adventure with God to follow Him in mission. One that will enable the Church to be all that she should be in relationship to God and one another as we form deeper relationships in Christian community, challenge the prevailing culture and introduce many to Jesus and his community – the Church. To know the love of the Father, follow the way of Jesus and live this out with one another in the power of the Spirit. It is a book calling us to be renewed in relationship, discipleship and the rediscovery of the adventure of mission as we 'model discipleship to unchurched people living out our lives with them in the spirit of Jesus' (p. 154, quote from a pioneer).

Rachel Jordan-Wolf
May 2019

Foreword

by Phil Potter

An axiom that I have lived and worked with for many years is the phrase 'Constant change is here to stay'. In a fast moving, complex, mobile and multicultured world, the old and simple certainties have long gone, and with them the assumption that our country is a Christian one (half of the UK population now has never had any experience of church whatsoever). My wife is a deputy head teacher in a local primary school on Merseyside, and every year she gets a graphic picture of an unchurched society. As Christmas comes around, she will often find that only a very small handful of five-year-olds have any concept of what the word 'Jesus' might mean at Christmas time. As she builds relationships with their families, she sees again and again that it is not only the parents who have never been to church, but actually the grandparents who form the first generation of completely unchurched people. For them, their children and children's children, their response to faith and Christian liturgy could be summed up in the words of a four-year-old child, who was overheard by a friend of mine saying her own version of the Lord's prayer: 'Our Father, who shouts from heaven, "Hello, what's your name?!"'

The Fresh Expressions movement was born out of a heartfelt desire by ordinary Christians to enable the world around them to discover God afresh, not as a distant supernatural stranger but an intimate Father who not only cares deeply about us, but makes his home with us and makes himself at home in a thousand different contexts. The stories in this book reflect that and are part of a worldwide movement that has been coming to terms with the fact that many people today just do not understand our church traditions, hymns, symbols and customs, because they have never been in contact with them. This is why growing numbers of churches are not only beginning to take what they do out of their building and into the community, but are completely reimagining it for those who don't do church. As they engage in this way with a vision to listen to both the context and to the Holy Spirit, they are delighted to rediscover for themselves the endless creativity of a God who welcomes all.

Across the movement and within these pages, you will see a blending of the old and the new, with the best of what is emerging alongside the wealth of what we have inherited as church. You will also see the ingredients that are helping us to develop new structures for church that are soft and flexible enough to overlay the present ones and help renew them. Think of it like a spider's web, something organic and fragile on the one hand yet strong and functional on the other. Like many fresh expressions of church, one thread on its own can look very fragile and vulnerable, of little use or worth perhaps, but a whole matrix of threads produces something strong, attractive and fit for purpose. The most encouraging thing in the Fresh Expressions story is that there are now many threads emerging. Most of them escape attention because they are just that – a thread. But a bigger picture is now emerging of a new movement of God that can effectively face the challenge of change in the twenty-first century. Follow the threads in this book, and you will find encouragement and inspiration for a new future for the Church that Christ will always love, and loves to see constantly changing.

Phil Potter
February 2019

Introduction

Life is full of being in the company of others. For some, depending upon temperament, mood and the company in which we find ourselves, this may seem to be either good news or bad. So, what will this book be? For it is a book about being in the company of others . . .

Over the past five years the Church of Scotland has been a partner of Fresh Expressions (UK), and this book is a reflection upon our experience during this time. It is not meant to be a formal treatise, but a thoughtful engagement with what has actually happened. We hope that lessons learnt and understanding gained by those involved in this form of mission will inspire and encourage all of us. We pray that their stories will help give us both confidence and an openness to share in what God is doing, as new forms of church communities develop. Our hope is that they will help us, wherever we may be,[1] identify and take the next step to which he is calling us.

The tone of this book is to let individuals and communities, as much as possible, speak for themselves. So, as well as my own observations drawn from conversation and reflection over the past five years, there is quite a bit of direct quotation from conversations, websites and written articles. This means that you will hear a wide variety of voices expressing themselves in different styles.[2]

The German poet Novalis[3] sought to make strange the familiar and to make familiar the strange – our fellow wayfarers are going to do the same. For those of us for whom familiarity has dulled the wonder of the church, they will help us see it afresh; they will help us catch the joy, the grace and the privilege of mission. For those of us for whom church is a foreign land, they will open up a map and guide us into new landscapes.

However, they will not beguile us into a world of wishful thinking and make-believe. Chalked on a board outside an Edinburgh pub, I saw the wisdom, 'Life is not a fairy tale: if you've lost your shoe at midnight then you're drunk'. In the stories, which we will hear, and the conversations in which we will share, there is a strong call to sober up and stop fooling ourselves. There is, also, a clear call to adventure.

Some of those whom we will meet as we journey through this book will speak, more directly, from the experience of their communities; this is mainly in Part 2.[4] Others, mainly in Part 3, will share with us key lessons that they have learnt as they have reflected, more generally, upon the development of fresh expressions of church in Scotland.

Part 1 briefly covers some basic ground on the thinking that undergirds fresh expressions of church. If you are already well acquainted with this and, as you begin to read this section, you feel like a granny being shown how to suck eggs, 'Pass Go' and move directly to Part 2.

As we begin, good words to recall are these:

Now to him[5] who is able to do immeasurably more than all we ask or imagine, according to his power that is at work within us, to him be glory in the church and in Christ Jesus throughout all generations for ever and ever. Amen. (Ephesians 3:20–1; NIV)

Notes

1 Although most of the examples cited are from Scotland, the experience reflected should be of relevance much further afield; this is not meant to be an introspective or chauvinistic account. For those who might find it helpful, Appendix 3 is a brief introduction to the Church of Scotland and to some of the terms or assumptions, which may have been mentioned or alluded to in interviews or articles (e.g. The Declaratory Act III helps us understand why the Church of Scotland

has a parish system and traditionally has had such a geographical focus on the development of Christian communities and mission in Scotland).

2 This will be, perhaps, most apparent in Part 3.

3 Novalis was the pseudonym for Georg Philipp Friedrich von Hardenberg (1772–1801) an author, philosopher and romantic poet and this maxim is often attributed to him. Another oft quoted remark of his is 'To romanticise the world is to make us aware of the magic, mystery and wonder of the world; it is to educate the senses to see the ordinary as extraordinary, the familiar as strange, the mundane as sacred, the finite as infinite' (quoted by Frederick C. Beiser in 'A Romantic Education: The Concept of Bildung in Early German Romanticism', in Rorty, Amélie (ed.), *Philosophers in Education: Historical Perspectives* (London: Routledge, 1998), p. 294).

4 These are primarily eight fresh expressions, or potential fresh expressions of church, which I interviewed in late 2017/early 2018. See Appendix 1 for more details of these groups.

5 Traditionally, the personal pronoun used when referring to God is masculine; however, this should not be seen as designating a defining gender to God. In this book I have, in general, used the noun God in preference to a personal pronoun. Where a pronoun has been needed, I wanted to avoid using 'it' as this has the connotation of the impersonal and often implies that which we control or seek to. My decision to use the masculine pronoun holds no implication that one gender more closely radiates the image of God, it simply acknowledges that in the Bible masculine imagery is used more often of God than feminine imagery (had the converse been true, I would have used the feminine pronoun).

Part 1

I

Fresh Expressions of Church:
Setting the Scene

In one of his stories for children, Oscar Wilde tells of a giant who has a beautiful walled garden, but, as he is a selfish giant, he will not let anyone visit this garden or enjoy its beauty. Over time he realises that, although the seasons come and go in the world around him, in his garden and in his house, it is always winter. Ice and frost reign, nothing will grow, and the garden is a wasteland of misery. One day, to his surprise, he sees some children sitting on the branches of the trees; they have crept in through a small hole in the wall. Then he notices something wonderful: the trees on which the children are sitting have begun to blossom and the ground around their roots is free from its carpet of hardened ice. Suddenly he understands and his heart is changed. In his selfishness, he has created this cage of despair: in denying love he has distorted what is natural, both within and without. He races to the street beyond the high walls of his garden and calls to the children of the town.

'It is your garden now, little children,' said the Giant, and he took an axe and knocked down the wall. And when the people were going to market they found the Giant playing with the children in the most beautiful garden they had ever seen.[1]

Moved from the winter of selfishness, the giant in Oscar Wilde's children's tale opens up to others not only his garden, but also his life. He changes dramatically as boundaries are broken down and ownership is shared. Yet, heart-warming as this story is, the giant continues to remain within the security and comfort of an invitation, one which he makes. But, what if something else had happened: what if he had left his garden to others and had travelled to places, fair or foul, where gardens were unknown, or at best only a plaintive imagining? What if he had shared his life with others by growing new gardens in different places? Now this 'going out and staying out', rather than 'going out and inviting back' is the story of fresh expressions of church.

It's good for us to stay, for a moment, with the giant and the children and to enjoy the great giving and receiving of life we see all around us; it helps us understand a real concern some have about what they perceive advocates of fresh expressions of church to be saying to the wider church. Justified or not, some perceive, from these advocates, an arrogance and a dismissal of others; the term 'fresh' is seen as implying that other expressions of church are 'stale' and second rate. The celebration in the garden helps us experience the joy when church in its inherited, more traditional expressions breaks down the walls, whatever they may be, and shares Jesus with others. Understandably, those who, through the power of the Holy Spirit, have reached out, engaged, invited others and then reconfigured their community accordingly feel hurt, devalued and even angry when both God's grace and their joy seem to be dismissed. At this point, it's important for us to highlight something that we are going to come across again and again: the importance of context and how a proper understanding of this is crucial if we are not to misinterpret one another. This sensitivity is also critical if we are to appropriately engage with communities in mission.

So, we need to explore where the term 'fresh' came from and what it was originally intended to express. This takes us back to 2004. The catalyst for the recent development of fresh expressions of church and the setting up of the Fresh Expression partnership (at least in the UK context) was the 'Mission-shaped Church' report within the Church of England.[2] As this report was discussed and built upon, it was natural, in an Anglican context, to refer to 'The Declaration of Assent', which all bishops, priests, deacons and readers agree to on their ordination or licensing. It states:

4

The Church of England is part of the One, Holy, Catholic and Apostolic Church worshipping the one true God, Father, Son and Holy Spirit. It professes the faith uniquely revealed in the Holy Scriptures and set forth in the catholic creeds, which faith the Church is called upon to proclaim *afresh* [my highlighting] in each generation. Led by the Holy Spirit, it has borne witness to Christian truth in its historic formularies, the Thirty-Nine Articles of Religion, the Book of Common Prayer and the Ordering of Bishops, Priests and Deacons. In the declaration you are about to make will you affirm your loyalty to this inheritance of faith as your inspiration and guidance under God in bringing the grace and truth of Christ to this generation and making Him known to those in your care?[3]

'Fresh', in 'fresh expressions of church', is from 'afresh' in this document; it is based upon the historic norm within the life and ministry of the Church of England: a norm of a sensitive and appropriate proclamation of the grace and truth of Christ to each generation. It is a statement of how God calls us to share in his mission; it is not a criticism of what is or what has been done. We'll look at this in more detail later, but from the beginning, those who have promoted fresh expressions of church have equally endorsed what they have called a mixed economy; that is they have validated the importance in mission of both inherited and fresh expressions of church.

In 2010, Rowan Williams, a former Archbishop of Canterbury and a strong, pioneer voice for the Fresh Expressions initiative, put it this way:

The mixed economy takes both elements seriously, both traditional forms of church and emerging forms of church, and I think it's very important that we don't nurture any illusion that there is only one really important bit of this. Needs are different in different contexts, and to say that partnership is the most promising mission strategy at the moment is to take both elements in the partnership seriously. It's tempting and easy to talk about 'the cutting edge' being in Fresh Expressions. The 'cutting edge', of course, is wherever people are brought into living relationship with Jesus Christ and when we think about how partnership best works, we must surely realise that it's when both elements are taking each other seriously and gratefully and interacting with each other. And I say that simply as a reminder to some who perhaps too readily either think that Fresh Expressions is everything, or on the other side who feel perhaps patronised or marginalised by the enthusiastic language about what's new. Working together creatively in partnership is indeed the most promising mission strategy.[4]

There is no implication that a 'go and invite back' approach is second class to a 'go and stay out' approach; there is only the acknowledgement of a mutual lack of monopoly. Both are important ways in which we, the Church, can engage in mission, but neither one is the only way forward.

Inherited and fresh expressions of church may engage in mission from different perspectives, but they are complementary streams of the Spirit's work and they should celebrate, support, comfort and challenge one another. We must never lose sight of this complementarity; we must not fall into a mire of false assumptions, fear, insecurity, jealousy or arrogance, which would hinder us from understanding better who God is and blind us from seeing what God is doing.

In our thinking together, let's pause for a moment. Something really important has been underscored for us: not just context, but the assumptions we make about context and about how others understand it. Within the Church of England, the term 'fresh' can be seen as a part of the ecclesiastical wallpaper; perhaps, at times, it needs to be pointed out, but it is easily visible and its significance understood. This is not necessarily the case for other traditions; within some of these, the term may have a negative connotation towards other forms of church and approaches to mission. This needs to be recognised, words and phrases need to be explained, contextualised, their significance understood by all and, where wise, reformulated. Genuine listening is fundamental to genuine communication and where all are honoured in this, then the seeds of community are sown.

We'll pick this up later, when we are thinking about how we begin to develop a fresh expression of church.

What is Church?

So far, so good, but, to date, we've been making an assumption: that we understand what church is. We have taken for granted that we agree upon this central identity, which both inherited and fresh expressions of church share. But, do we?

What is the first thing that comes to mind when we hear, or read, the word church; not our considered opinion, but the first impression? Is it a building, a group of people, a practice, an experience, a relationship or something else? What is it about this first impression that gave it such priority? Even if our considered opinion as to what church is would be amplified, more nuanced or quite different, does this gut reaction still have a role to play in our personal understanding of church? Complexity once again weaves strands together as our understanding of church is not just an intellectual definition, it is an emotional reaction as well and, depending on our experience, our understanding of spirituality and our sense of identity may well be woven into the mix.

A particularly sensitive area is how we understand specific practices that churches enact or live out. These practices could vary from the sacramental to the setting out and allocation of seats; from the form of worship to the tea rota; from the role of each person within the church community to the implicit dress code. A helpful question to ask is what, if any, specific form of practice is essential to being a church community? Now, we're not thinking here about general areas of practice (e.g. gathering for worship), but the specific form which that practice must take (e.g. gathering together at 11.00 a.m. on a Sunday morning). At this point, some of us may find ourselves surprised, for although we might identify general areas of practice, we haven't been able to identify any essential, specific form for a practice. So, for example if we think about sacraments: most, if not all, church traditions are sacramental,[5] but some traditions practise seven, others two and others have no specific designated sacraments as they see all of life as sacramental. Even in those traditions that practise baptism and Holy Communion/Breaking of Bread, there is often not only a difference in action, but also in theological nuance. This openness and variety of specific practice is to be expected because of what church is in its essence.

So then, what is church? Church, in both its inherited and fresh expressions, is a gift from God. It is enlivened by the Holy Spirit and given to us by the Father through Jesus who leads it. It is deeply and fundamentally relational: it is 'One, Holy, Catholic and Apostolic'. These relationships through Jesus form a matrix as we relate to one another in unity and fellowship, to God in dependence upon his grace, to the Church universal through time and space and to our communities and wider world in mission. Church in its essence is relational, and any practices we have, either in a general or a specific sense, must serve the relationships we have through Jesus. If practices move outside of, or become independent of, or take priority over these relationships, then they lead the way to idolatry.

Let's re-enter the company of Rowan Williams:

we need to have a clear and robust understanding of what the church really is. It is not in the New Testament a carefully constructed human society, organising itself in local branches, with members signing up to a constitution. Instead, it is what happens when the news and presence of Jesus, raised from the dead, impact upon the human scene, drawing people together in a relationship that changes everyone involved, a relationship which means that each person involved with Jesus is now involved with all others who have answered his invitation, in ways that can be painful and demanding, but also life-giving and transforming beyond imagination.[6]

Church is a 'space', where in the company of others we encounter the risen Jesus Christ and are transformed by him, and through him we enter the treasure of relationships that we mentioned earlier. Relationship is central to being church.

What Is a Fresh Expression of Church?

If church, whatever its particular form of expression, is essentially this relational matrix, in what way or ways is this nuanced in a fresh expression of church: an expression of church that is intentionally missional, contextual and focused on discipleship? Let's visit some examples.

Once in the thrall of the reivers' raid and romanticised by Sir Walter Scott, the Scottish Borders fire the imagination. They are a place of changing contour, wood and river, a place where mystery seems easily present and adventure bids a welcome. In 2011, a particular venture, 'Gateways', began in the small village of Paxton.

Gateways is a fresh expression of church, initiated by and developed within the parish of Hutton, Fishwick and Paxton. It is a rural community church serving the parish and surrounding Scottish Borders and Northumberland area:

> Based around our values of hope, creativity and inclusivity Gateways exists to build Christian community and share the timeless good news message of Jesus Christ in a relevant way.[7]

Their life together highlights what is core to so many fresh expressions of church: genuine hospitality, which allows relationships to blossom and life to flow.

Fresh expressions of church are self-consciously focused on keeping central the relationships that we have in and through Jesus. Appropriate practices are seen to develop from the outworking of these relationships. The community of the church is therefore not essentially defined by specific practices or a theological tradition, though practices and theological expressions consonant with these core relationships will develop and indeed some may be shared across time, geography and a variety of cultures.

A second characteristic shared by many fresh expressions of church is the process through which they have developed. The experience and reflection of many pioneers has identified an

organic process, which strongly resonates with our best practice of cross-cultural mission.

Now here we need to be very careful, as all too easily we
could move into assuming formulaic, off-the-shelf answers.
This identified process is not a neat, linear progression, which
like a train (if it were running to timetable) would take us from
A to B, with the requisite in-between stops called at on schedule
and the waiting passengers duly picked up. No, this is messier
and more life-givingly jumbled. It is a process that is saturated
in prayer and where the community in mission can be at peace
with its vulnerability and limitations; it is a process with the
default awareness that this mission is God's mission and that
we are given the gift of sharing in this: it is not our possession.

A helpful way to think of this process is as a series of ongoing interactions, which have a non-prescriptive staggered start
and which augment and complement one another.

The first part of this process is often, what is sometimes termed,
a 'holy disquiet'. It is not necessarily that the life of a church
community is problematic; it is that the community, or some in
the community, sense that there is something more, something
'as well' in which God is calling them to share. Gradually, they
begin to sense a new context of mission and then some go and
begin to engage with this new setting. In their going, they com-
mit to stay; they intend to develop a church community in this
new context. If the intention is to engage people, draw them
back and welcome them into the sending community (even a
'reconfigured' one), this, as we have said, while being an entirely
valid form of mission engagement, is not a fresh expression of
church.

Let's meet a group in the north-east of Scotland in the city
of Aberdeen; a city of granite, academia, northern lights, oil
and once a contender as the future birthplace of 'Scotty' from
Star Trek. To the north of the city lies Stockethill, an area that
developed primarily as a postwar community in the late 1940s.
In 1949, the foundation stone for the building of the new
church Extension Charge was laid. In the Church of Scotland,
Church Extension was a form of mission where a contemporary expression of church was 'planted' in a new community.

The assumption was that across Scotland there was sufficient cultural homogeneity that an expression of church from one context would, with a certain degree of customising, automatically resonate in a new context. At times, this appeared to be true, so 'Many remember a thriving time for the church during the seventies . . . when the building was at the centre of many community activities and was the hub for a diversely aged and friendly church.'[8]

However, this did not continue, and half a century after its enthusiastic inauguration Stockethill parish faced a crisis and an opportunity:

> By the late nineties, the church had fallen on harder times. The few who were left in the church were exhausted from the responsibility of running the church and maintaining the building. The presbytery might have been expected to dissolve the congregation or unite it with another parish church. However, conversations were taking place in the Church of Scotland about how to restart churches that had come to an end: 'brown field' New Charge Development.[9]

New Charge Development was one particular way (although the term was not being used at the time) that the Church of Scotland was experimenting with and developing fresh expressions of church within communities.

> New Charge Development was formed as a way of giving space for new parish churches to develop and emerge in a way that was right for their community. There was to be space and freedom given for a community of faith to develop in a sensitive responsiveness to the particular civic community they found themselves in and so to find a form of church that was best suited to the people in that community. Churches could grow up, each as unique as the community in which they were birthed.[10]

The new expression of church, in Stockethill, grew and blossomed, yet, in the midst of this celebration a 'holy disquiet' and sensitive discontent was stirring. Some began to feel uneasy with the church's 'chaplaincy' model of engagement with those in sheltered accommodation within the parish. It wasn't that these folk were not genuinely loved and cared for and invited to be a part of all that the new church community was doing and becoming; it was something else.

> One common traditional approach of the church in its engagement with older people, particularly those in sheltered or supported accommodation, has been to care for them through visiting and, if possible, to provide opportunities for worship through a monthly short service. The limitations of this approach are at least two-fold.
>
> First, it perpetuates the form of church that in many cases has already been rejected over the course of a life by those outside of the church, and so has limited missional impact.
>
> Second, the services and visits tend to be implicitly understood by those conducting the services and those attending as a second-class form of church: the elderly are cared for in this approach, they are not treated, included in the full life of the church.
>
> There is a need, therefore, for new forms of church which offer to the world a powerful counter-cultural witness to the kingdom of God through a refusal to view the elderly as a secondary part of the Church. Instead, we wish to include them as essential members of the body of Christ, alongside others drawn from every age of life.[11]

And so, from one fresh expression of church another was birthed: Neither Young Nor Old (NYNO), '[a] fresh expression of multi-generational church amongst older people, particularly, but not exclusively, those who live in sheltered housing accommodation'.[12]

Rupert Holmes's song 'Escape (The Piña Colada Song)' was the last US Number One hit of 1979. It tells of a man who, bored with his partner, answers an advertisement in a newspaper to meet someone who, from their wish list, seems to share both his likes in life and his sense of fun. When he arrives at the designated bar both parties are surprised, for his date is none other than his present partner.

Irony and a barbed reality check, not only for romantic relationships, but for much of life. How often do we live on the silt of false assumptions because we have not listened to the other? How often do we understand too little because we assume too much? The second stage highlighted in the development of fresh expressions of church is 'active listening'. Of course, listening to God and to the local church community has been a part of the process from the beginning, but what is being underscored here is deep, humble listening to the new context and the moving of our assumed understanding to the 'provisional' or 'tentative' category.

As we listen to God and to the new context, we must not assume that we understand this new culture. Genuine openhearted, open-minded and open-spirited listening is essential, and this will change not only us, but our understanding and our actions.

Think for a moment of two significant political events in 2016: the result of the Brexit referendum in the UK, on whether to remain in the European Union, and the election of Donald Trump as the forty-fifth President of the United States of America. Why were so many surprised when the votes were counted? As we will remind ourselves again and again, life is complex and we must avoid being naively simplistic, and so it is with the above events. However, part of the dynamic at play was that one group made assumptions about the value of the opinion of another. A section of society felt voiceless, sidelined and dismissed by the other, and it reacted to this when the opportunity arose.

J. D. Vance writes about his turn-of-millennium childhood and early adult life in *Hillbilly Elegy*. He invites us into the company of his family and his community; a community which in the USA seems to be not only marginalised, but misunderstood; a community that not only has its own norms, but also had its own way to distribute justice. He tells of someone, in his family's home area of Breathitt, who, suspected of rape, was executed by the community; and this with impunity from wider society.

One of the most common tales of Breathitt's lore revolved around an older man who was accused of raping a young girl . . . days before his trial the man was found face down in a local lake with sixteen bullet wounds in his back. The authorities never investigated the murder, and the only mention of the incident appeared in the local newspaper on the morning his body was discovered. In an admirable display of journalistic pith, the paper reported: 'Man found dead. Foul play suspected.' 'Foul play expected?' my grandmother would roar. 'You're goddamned right. Bloody Breathitt got to that son of a bitch.'[13]

It's a world that most don't comprehend, because they have never walked through that landscape or listened to those who shape and are shaped by it. Two of the many comments he makes are important for us to hear at this point.

The first concerns when, in the mid-twentieth century, many hillbillies migrated to urban areas in the Midwest. They deeply disturbed local sensibilities – it wasn't just that as rural people they seemed out of place in an urban context, but rather,

these migrants disrupted a broad set of assumptions held by northern whites about how white people appeared, spoke and behaved . . . the disturbing aspect of hillbillies was their racialness. Ostensibly they were of the same racial order (whites) as those who dominated economic, political and social power in local and national arenas. But hillbillies shared many regional characteristics with the southern blacks arriving in Detroit.[14]

Second, he laments that when wider society tries to help his community it often fails, not due to a lack of good intentions and compassion, but due to its ignorance and lack of comprehension. In fact, it can, in his opinion, end up doing more harm than good.[15]

This is a sober call not just to society in general, but to us as church as we share the extravagant love of God. We'll look at this in more detail in Part 3, but let's take note that this deep, active, respectful and reflective listening and the appreciation and understanding that arise from it is fundamental to what often develops next in the story of a fresh expression of church: loving service.

As we listen to those in this new context, we begin to integrate into a community and to understand how this community can best be loved and served. Without pretence, we begin to do this more as 'insiders' rather than 'outsiders' who have been parachuted in.

The fortunes of cities often ebb and flow, and the coastal city of Dundee is no exception. It is Scotland's fourth-largest city; the population is just over 148,000 and it lies on the north bank of the Firth of Tay as the river flows towards the North Sea. It has a strong maritime, industrial and publishing history, but suffered severe decline during the latter part of the twentieth century. Now, however, it is developing into a prestigious cultural and university centre. It has a high reputation in biomedical sciences and in the world of comics, graphic novels and video games (*Grand Theft Auto* was developed there). A new V&A Museum has opened on the waterfront. In the centre of the city is a large shopping complex which arcs around The Steeple – an old church (present building from 1789) and a grassy plaza area. In 2001, something new began in this area: 'Hot Chocolate'.

For decades, the grass outside The Steeple Church has been the meeting place for young people who often feel they don't quite belong in their own local communities or schools.

Back in 2001, The Steeple Church was noticing that two communities – theirs inside and the young folk's outside – were living side by side and never interacting. So a wee group left the shelter of their walls to get to try to know the young folks. This group didn't have any agendas other than to build a bit of relationship. But since it was November and cold, what they did have was Hot Chocolate, which was what the young people started calling these interactions . . .

Over the course of the following weeks, relationships started growing, trust started building, and dreams started emerging, until the question was asked: 'If you had a wee bit of space within the building, what would you want to use it for?' And so the growing community began moving indoors and gradually expanded into the well-established independent organisation it is now.

Since the outset, it has been the young people who have made the decisions about how, when and what happens. These roots remain totally foundational to who we are and the way we operate today . . .[16]

Hot Chocolate exemplifies the going out, staying and active listening that is critical for appropriate loving service to develop. It's interesting to note that although they invited the new community, which they were serving, back into their church building, they did not invite them back into their church culture: they were developing a fresh expression of church in the same physical space, but a different cultural one.

By their nature, relationships are not always predictable, their fortunes too can ebb and flow; for Hot Chocolate, there was a waxing and not a waning. Their loving service, lived out as part of a community, birthed another community within this wider cultural group. Not a closed, hermetically sealed silo, but an open house, which was home to an ever-growing family. 'First and foremost Hot Chocolate is not here to do things for young people. We are not here to provide a service for young people, but instead to grow a community with young people. That subtle difference actually makes all the difference.'[17] Crucially, those who initiated Hot Chocolate are a wholehearted part of this community, which has developed from their loving service.

Now we come to something that, although we all agree is mandatory, can easily be perceived as a spanner in the works or the elephant in the room: discipleship. Discipleship is a term that we can use in referring to both 'being a disciple' and the 'making of disciples', and although the experience of being a disciple and discipling was a common reality in the world of Jesus, the term discipleship is not without its difficulties in our present world. Once again, we'll think more about this later, but in setting the scene it's important for us to be aware that for some, discipleship can seem a hurdle. A hurdle not just in the sense that we all struggle with the integrity of our own living as bearers of Christ's name, but in the sense of fearing that discipleship and discipling, in particular, is artificial to the relationships that we are building. I find that when talking with churches and groups about the development of a fresh expression of church, they may easily see how listening, loving, serving and building community can develop, but somehow there seems a gulf between these and discipleship; somehow, for many, discipleship appears almost as an impertinent imposition, which we sneak in through the back door. Before we put our thinking about this on hold, there are a few important things to keep in mind.

First, we, as individuals and as a church community must always be open and honest about who we are. This is part of the integrity of the level playing field which we want to establish: we want everyone to move from the fear of pretence to the freedom of honesty. True, our Christian identity may not be the first thing we share with a new acquaintance, that could be artificial, but we should live out wholeheartedly who we are and as such express naturally our faith in word, thought and action. When it comes to developing partnerships in the community, we assure people that we will not abuse relationships or use the partnership as a back door to 'proselytise', but equally we will never deny who we, individual or church community, are. We will see people as whole people, and this includes the spiritual; with integrity, we will engage with them as such. It may seem a fine balance, but it is the natural outworking of our walking with Jesus.

Following from this, we need to be confident that the Spirit of Jesus within us will be evident as we get on with the normal business of everyday life. The key is our wanting to be and become the person and the community that Jesus wants us to be, despite our messing it up at times. For a moment, let's imagine ourselves at a party. It's a great party, the room is crowded, everyone is having a good time and the glasses have just been filled. Suddenly, at the far side of the room, you spot an old friend and you start to move towards them.

As you enthusiastically wend your way, someone coming in the opposite direction bumps into you and in the slight jostle you both spill some of your drink. As no-one is drunk and it's a friendly party, there is no problem; it's just one of those things that can happen when lots of people are together enjoying themselves. However, what's important for us is that whatever was in each of the glasses, be it soft drink, wine or beer, is what will spill. It is the same with us in everyday life: as we are with people in the normal jostle of life, whatever is within us will overflow. If the Spirit of Jesus is within us, that is what will spill out; that is what will be evident. We don't have to contrive this, so we can relax.

Finally, when people encounter Jesus, there is always the opportunity for change and transformation, even before a person may recognise who he is. So, in a way, the formation of disciples may be happening from the very beginning, though it is likely to become more intentional as relationships and community develop.

As the dynamic we've been thinking about develops (probably with a quantum rather than a Newtonian sense of orderliness),[18] a new expression of church may emerge. This community will be true to what church is in its essence and to the realities of the cultural context in which it is being expressed. It may well be that we are unclear when this development takes place, but what will be clear is that we are now part of a new, albeit fragile, church community. Sean Stillman, a leader in Zac's Place, a fresh expression of church in Swansea, says:

> The transition from just meeting like a mission gathering . . . to becoming a church; (it) is actually difficult to know where that transition takes place. I can't pinpoint a time when Zac's Place: church in a pub, with a question mark, lost its question mark. But, I know, as I look back, at some stage the community of faith, which has become Zac's Place developed, matured and has grown into something that functions as a loving and caring community that wants to serve and follow Jesus. I don't think that was an overnight thing, but the whole process of wanting to serve people on the margins, wanting to journey together, wanting to be honest and real with each other, that has produced that kind of bond and that sort of community together.[19]

No fresh expression of church is an end in itself: mission should be intrinsic to its DNA and explicit in its living of life. So, in time, just as in Stockethill, some from a fresh expression of church should go and develop a new expression of church in a new context.

Fresh or Froth Expressions of Church?

An important concern that is often and legitimately raised is: Are fresh expressions of church merely a pragmatic quick fix or are they a profound expression of God's grace and love? Are they deeply and fundamentally grounded in our understanding of God; God who loves, sacrifices and reigns?

We do need to take these questions seriously, particularly as in our culture and society, even though there are many wonderful things about it, there are significant influences that would blind us to the difference between technique and relationship, appearance and substance. A helpful way to weigh this up is to think about four realities that are central to our Christian faith: Trinity, Incarnation, Kingdom of God and the 'Wildness of God'. If these realities are foundational in the development of a fresh expression of church and radiated in its ongoing life, then there is substance not froth. Let's take a moment to ponder these realities, which cannot but move us to wonder and humility.

Trinity

Where do we begin as we reflect upon this mystery that helps us see so much? Here we can only mention a few thoughts and indicate how they begin to relate to fresh expressions of church.

First, there is diversity in utter unity of being. Second, there is uncompromised love, which is mutually and equally given and received. Third, we witness the reality of communication. Fourth, we see communion-in-mission (or community-in-mission).[20] These qualities are at the core of reality, and if a church, whether traditional or fresh, national, local or denominational in its expression is to have integrity, it must not just reflect, but radiate these qualities.

A fresh expression of church intentionally aims to integrate these qualities of life into its DNA. It explicitly understands church in relational terms. These relationships are comprehensive and are focused in and through Jesus. There is an unapologetic attempt to model communion-in-mission: where love is mutually given and received and where it is uncompromisingly expressed to others.

There is a deep appreciation and exploration of diversity and unity. This is reflected in all being encouraged not just to use the gifts and experience that God has given them, but to radically live out the 'priesthood of all believers'. John 14—17 speaks of the Trinity in action and how all are where the one is. How do we understand delegation and representation in the light of this? What does this say about service, discipling, the delegation of the administration of the sacraments and our understanding of the 'ordained'/'lay' dynamic? Fresh expressions of church explore how the reality of this interdependent relationship should shape our practice, rather than letting inherited practices become principles by which we interpret our relationships.

Communication is understood, not just in intellectual terms, but in and through the reality of relationship; it is expected that God will make himself known, in new contexts, through the integration of our presence, words and actions as we be with one another in these settings.

Incarnation

George Lings, former director of the Church Army's Research Unit, is someone who has studied and thought deeply about fresh expressions of church. In his teaching and in his book *Reproducing Churches*,[21] he makes the, perhaps provocative, suggestion that the incarnation of Jesus was a fresh expression of the Second Person of the Trinity: the existence and experience of Jesus of Nazareth was different from the existence and experience of God the Son prior to this. In this, the Son's divinity was not compromised, yet neither was the humanity, which had been, and was, active in shaping this new expression of identity. If this is true, it has significant implications for how we understand our identity as church and how our engagement with a context should shape the expression of church.

Philippians 2:1–11 speaks of the humility and love of Jesus and calls us to follow his example. It speaks of Jesus truly becoming one of us, not just pretending. This means that the context had a significant role in the expression of the incarnation. A fresh expression of church takes both this radical humility and the significance of context as central to mission. In the incarnation, neither divinity nor humanity were compromised, so in a fresh expression of church neither the integrity of being church nor the cultural context will be compromised. We need not fear when the context is given its rightful place and is allowed to be an active agent in shaping an expression of church, as this is the only way to follow the model of the incarnation.

Landlocked in central Italy, in the region of Umbria, rests the town of Assisi. At the turn of the thirteenth century, it faced a crisis and was at war with the neighbouring town of Perugia. In 1202, after Assisi lost the battle of Collestrada, we meet one soldier from Assisi who, imprisoned for a year, is soon to face a crisis of his own. His father, a wealthy cloth merchant, pays his ransom and probably expects his offspring to return to soldiering and his relatively carefree life, which to an extent he apparently does. However, something else is going on: deep discontent and searching. A pilgrimage to Rome in 1205 begins a process that culminates a few years later when our now former soldier and prisoner receives a radical clarity.

One morning at Mass, he hears the reading of the day from Matthew 10:7–10; the point in the life of the twelve apostles where Jesus instructs them to,

'Go . . . preach, "The Kingdom of Heaven is near," heal the sick, raise the dead, cleanse those who have leprosy, drive out demons. Freely you have received, freely give. Do not take any gold or silver or copper in your belts, take no bag for the journey, or extra tunic, or sandals or a staff, for the worker is worth his keep.' (NIV)

He is affirmed in his setting aside of wealth and prestige to follow a life of poverty, caring for the sick and preaching the good news of love and repentance. His name, of course, is Francis and he later summarised his way of life as 'to follow the teaching and footprints of our Lord Jesus Christ'.[22]

Francis knew that to follow Jesus would mean a relinquishing of power coupled with a willingness to accept sacrifice in our active loving of others; this is the way of the incarnation. It underscores that our motivation for developing a fresh expression of church is not one of seeking power, maintaining prestige or guarding comfort; it is one of love, love for the other, especially love for the one who is not already included. In this, our identity is neither self-centred nor self-denying.

George Lings helpfully reminds us that the incarnation is not a static, siloed event: we understand it, not only in the context of the history of Israel, but in the context of the life, death, resurrection, ascension and expected return of Jesus, with all that is implied in this for the 'new heaven and the new earth'. We now relate to the post-resurrection Jesus; we are part of the body of the risen, ascended Jesus.[23] Time, place and the flow of life are important. Further, the incarnation of the Second Person of the Trinity was a unique event, so we must be suitably circumspect when we apply its example to our life. All of this, however, does not take away from the main point we're thinking about: the God-given basis, or foundation, of fresh expressions of church. In the development of fresh expressions of church, we experience a clear resonance with the incarnation: its love, integrity, glory and sacrifice.

Kingdom of God

From his books, it would seem hard to be in the company of Tom Wright without being enthused about the 'kingdom of God' and proclaiming the 'good news' of Jesus.[24] He celebrates the wonder of this kingdom and the glory of the life, death, resurrection and ascension of Jesus, which heralds the new heaven and the new earth and underscores its reality.

True, the full expression of this kingdom is in our future, but it must radically inform how we live and be church today. The death, mourning, suffering, injustice and evil of the 'old order of things', which John highlights for us in his vision,[25] need to be challenged today, at a practical level and not merely a theoretical one.

This, of course, can only be done as we engage with the reality of people's worlds in the contexts in which they live their everyday life. Loving service, which is aimed at transformation, not just relief, is central to this and is intentionally expressed within fresh expressions of church.

Further, there is a particular way in which the perspective, focus and intention of fresh expressions of church declare the kingdom of God. By developing expressions of church in new contexts, we consciously work for the kingdom of God to be expressed and experienced in these contexts, rather than calling people to experience it elsewhere. This deeply reflects the reality that Jesus is King in every context and not just in those cultures in which there are already expressions of church. To not have the heart and vision to go and seek to develop new expressions of church, which resonate with and are within the cultures in which they are to be found is, implicitly, to deny that Jesus can be Lord of that culture: we are saying that the kingdom of God is limited by human ingenuity.

'Wildness of God'

This phrase may seem strange, but let's journey with C. S. Lewis to the Land of Narnia:

> 'Aslan a man!' said Mr Beaver sternly. 'Certainly not. I tell you he is the King of the wood and the son of the great Emperor-beyond-the Sea. Don't you know who is the King of Beasts? Aslan is a lion – the Lion, the great Lion.'
>
> 'Ooh!' said Susan, 'I'd thought he was a man. Is he – quite safe? I shall feel rather nervous about meeting a lion.'

'That you will, dearie, and no mistake,' said Mrs Beaver; 'if there is one who can appear before Aslan without their knees knocking, either they're braver than most or just plain silly.'

'Then he isn't safe?' said Lucy.

'Safe?' said Mr Beaver, 'don't you hear what Mrs Beaver tells you? Who said anything about safe? 'Course he isn't safe. But he's good. He's the King, I tell you.'[26]

'He (Aslan) is not the slave of the stars, but their Maker. Is it not said in all the old stories that He is not a tame lion.'[27]

The phrase isn't a strange one, because it reminds us of a reality that, too often we, as individuals and as a church community, would readily run away from; for a variety of reasons, we are tempted to try and domesticate God. We, like Susan and Lucy, when they first hear of Aslan, misunderstand safety. We too readily exchange the anchor of God's goodness for the flotsam of our own wisdom. We let fear take its unrightful place, and although the adventure of mission calls us to both risk and to an openness to sacrifice, we forget that it does so in the context of love; love that is equally for us and for others. This is a perfect love, which drives out fear and allows no element of it remain.[28]

Fresh expressions of church celebrate this wildness and the call inspired by it; they intentionally cultivate a seeking of the presence and action of God in the wild, open seas of our world, not just in the inland waters of the well-mapped.

If we try and control God we miss what He is doing even if we are wanting to be more discerning. All of us can deceive ourselves, so there is no room to point the finger.[29]

When read in a place of comfort and peace, the above sounds reasonable, even motivating, but life, we know, isn't always an abode of ease and a haven of rest. At times, the storm thunders and we lash ourselves to the mast, unsure if we will survive, but deep down certain that there is no other course to sail.

The price of encountering reality, we might say, is precisely the recognition that there isn't an alternative to it. And the challenge is whether we can believe that, often in spite of appearances, it is the wellspring of joy. Hardest of all is when the very vehicles of faith or trust seem to become empty . . . and how it is necessary to hold on to what may feel like – at best – a deeply uncertain vision, haunted by all the ingenious ways in which it can be distorted and turned into falsehood.[30]

Move now to the city of Jerusalem, and we meet a group who are struggling to understand what it means to follow God: God who is untameable and who delights in giving birth to fresh expressions of church (Acts 15:1–35). We have travelled back in time, almost 2,000 years from our present, and we are witnessing the early days of the church; the stakes could hardly be higher. Heartfelt opinions, which deeply reflect not only believers' theological perspectives, but their deep sense of identity, are being expressed.

Something has happened; everyone gathered knows that it is the work of God, but what to make of it is another matter. Gentiles have received the Holy Spirit; they are a part of the church, but what must they do to show, if not their legitimacy, their honouring, perhaps even worthiness, of this new inheritance? The church community had, naturally enough, initially developed from within the Jewish culture, and as such they continued to hold those practices which God had given their people through the law. For us, travelling to meet them in their time and place, we must see this through their eyes and feel the weight of the struggle which is in their hearts. We mustn't clinically observe it as an exchange of philosophical propositions. Identity, integrity and the honouring of God are centre stage. How could God go back on what he had said? How could anyone's relationship with him deepen if they ignore his word? What did it mean to develop a true and full expression of church in this alien landscape and heartland? What, if any, practices should they demand of this new community if they were to be considered a worthy part of the true church?

Remember, we aren't thinking of 'a problem' of the Jewish church's making, but of a turmoil that has been created by the wild, undomesticated, at times unpredictable and uncomfortable God who cannot be tamed and whose Spirit will blow where God wishes. No-one is God's advisor. So what did they conclude about the nature of grace and of the church?

They discerned and affirmed three key aspects of reality. First, God, who will not conform to our expectations or comfort, is Lord of the church (vv. 7–18).

Second, that being part of the church is a gift of grace. We share in this new community because of the relationship we have with God, through Jesus; not through adherence to traditional or cultural religious practices. Throughout history, the initiative of relationship was with God, and God alone knew what practices, at any one time, would significantly help those in a particular culture develop and deepen their relationship with him (vv. 8–11). They realised that practices were to serve relationships and that because of the radicalness of all that was entailed in the good news of Jesus, new ways of living were now called into being. This did not deny the validity or importance of what had previously best served their people in knowing God and in serving him; it was just that a new age had dawned. As crawling is the way for a caterpillar to move and flying for a butterfly, so the world had changed for the people of God.

Third, they recognised and celebrated this new cultural diversity and freedom; with enthusiasm they prioritised mutual respect, encouragement and fellowship between the different expressions of church (vv. 22–34).

A Benediction for the Whole Church

There is much more we could think about as we set the scene for our exploration of fresh expressions of church, but let's leave it here as we join the company of fellow apprentices of Jesus and hear their stories. Recall again the words of Ephesians 3, which we mentioned at the end of the Introduction – words which are both a benediction and a challenging declaration of and for the whole church, whatever its expression: inherited or fresh. Across time, place and culture, they call us to celebrate and live out the radical gift of being church; it is indeed a good place to both finish and to begin.

Now to him who is able to do more than all we ask or imagine, according to his power that is at work within us, to him be glory in the church and in Christ Jesus throughout all generations, for ever and ever! Amen. (Ephesians 3:20–1; NIV)

Notes

1 'The Selfish Giant' by Oscar Wilde, in *The Complete Works of Oscar Wilde* (Glasgow: Geddes and Grosset, 2001), p. 116.

2 *Mission-Shaped Church* (Norwich: Church House Publishing, 2004).

3 The Book of Common Prayer.

4 'Mission-shaped Church', Report from the Mission and Public Affairs Council, Tuesday 9 February 2010; a contribution from the Archbishop of Canterbury, Dr Rowan Williams, at the General Synod, London; from Dr Rowan Williams 104th Archbishop of Canterbury, available online at http://aoc2013.brix.fatbeehive.com/articles.php/1955/mission-shaped-church-report-from-the-mission-and-public-affairs-council.

5 Some ecclesiologies, e.g. Baptist, would use other terminology to express their theological perspective of what are perceived as sacraments within other traditions: baptism and Communion are ordinances, not sacraments, although there may, at times, be a gap between 'official' doctrine and popular practice and understanding. Other groups such as the Salvation Army would see, or could be argued as seeing, all of life as sacramental.

6 Rowan Williams, Mixed Economy, Issue 1 (Autumn/Winter 2008/2009), p. 13. Also available online at https://institute.wycliffecollege.ca/2009/02/the-'strength'-of-the-church-is-never-anything-other-than-the-strength-of-the-presence-of-the-risen-jesus/.

7 Gateways website, www.gatewaysfellowship.co.uk.

8 Stockethill website, www.stockethillchurch.org.uk.

9 Stockethill website.

10 Stockethill website.

11 NYNO website, www.nyno.org.uk.

12 NYNO website.

13 Vance, J. D., *Hillbilly Elegy: A Memoir of a Family and Culture in Crisis* (New York: HarperCollins, 2016), pp. 16–17.

14 Obermiller, Philip J., Thomas E. Wagner and E. Bruce Tucker, *Appalachian Odyssey: Historical Perspectives on the Great Migration*

(Westport, CT: Praeger, 2000), p. 145. Quoted in Vance, *Hillbilly Elegy*, p. 31.

15 Vance, *Hillbilly Elegy*, pp. 241–4.

16 Hot Chocolate website, www.hotchocolate.org.uk.

17 Hot Chocolate website.

18 In Newtonian mechanics, the interactions of reality are understood to be ordered in such a way that if all the factors are known exact prediction is possible. However, in quantum mechanics, randomness is a built-in factor of reality and as such although statistically significant prediction can be made, especially at the macro-level, precise universal prediction is intrinsically impossible.

19 'Zac's Place' video (2012) Fresh Expressions website, https://freshexpressions.org.uk.

20 Bevans, Stephen B. and Schroeder, Roger P., *Constants in Context: A Theology for Mission Today* (Maryknoll, NY: Orbis, 2004), quoted by Michael Moynagh in *Church for Every Context* (London: SCM Press, 2012) pp. 140–6, where he argues that this is more integrated than community-in-mission and is more likely to avoid tritheism. George Lings in *Reproducing Churches* (Abingdon: BRF, 2017), pp. 76–9, argues for the use of community-in-mission, but acknowledges that there are considerations and arguments for both phrases. Behind both terms he states, 'are the sense of being communal and the assertion that God, and thus humans and also the church, share this sort of being, which is based on relations' (p. 79).

21 Lings, *Reproducing Churches*, pp. 99–100.

22 St Francis of Assisi, *Regula non bullata* (Earlier Rule), I.1, available online at www.franciscantradition.org/francis-of-assisi-early-documents/the-saint/writings-of-francis/the-earlier-rule/78-fa-ed-1-page-63.

23 Lings, *Reproducing Churches*, particularly chapters 5 and 6.

24 These themes recur in much of his writing as Tom Wright and N. T. Wright, e.g. *Surprised by Hope* (London: SPCK, 2007), *Simply Good News* (London: SPCK, 2015), *The Day the Revolution Began* (London: SPCK, 2016).

25 Revelation 21:4.

26 Lewis, C. S., *The Lion, the Witch and the Wardrobe*, p. 146, in *The Complete Chronicles of Narnia* (Collins, 1998).

27 Lewis, C. S., *The Last Battle*, p. 677, in *The Complete Chronicles of Narnia* (Collins, 1998).

28 1 John 4:18.

29 Hot Chocolate interview.

30 Williams, Rowan, *The Lion's World* (London: SPCK, 2012), p. 70.

Part 2
Introduction

At the beginning of *Mr Standfast*, Richard Hannay, the hero of some of John Buchan's most famous stories, is nursing anger and resentment. He is feeling sorry for himself. It is 1917 and he has been recalled from the front to, once again, enter the world of espionage, and he is not a happy man. As he considers backing away from this challenge, three things happen: he visits a friend whose mind has been shattered by the shell and shock of war; he reads a letter from a comrade who is now a prisoner of war and crippled in body; and he finds himself sitting on a ridge surveying the English countryside – wood, meadow, stream and village stretch below. A transformation takes place:

> In that moment I had a kind of revelation. I had a vision of what I had been fighting for, what we had been fighting for. It was peace, deep and holy and ancient, peace older than the oldest wars, peace which would endure when all our swords were hammered into ploughshares. It was more, for in that hour England first took hold of me. Before my country had been South Africa . . . But now I realised I had a new home wholly worth striving for . . . in that hour I had a prospect as if from a hilltop which made all the present troubles of the road seem of no account. I saw not only victory after war, but a new and happier world after victory, when I should inherit something of this English peace and wrap myself in it till the end of my days.[1]

Hannay realises his whole perspective and understanding of life had been distorted by the blinkered focus of life in the trenches; he had lost not only vision, but, in a way, life itself.

> my whole being had found a new purpose. Living in the trenches, you are apt to get your horizon narrowed down to the front line of the enemy barbed wire on one side and the nearest rest billets on the other. But now I seemed to see beyond the fog to a happy country.[2]

A century on, we may look back at Hannay's hope with wistfulness and sorrow, but this hindsight shouldn't blind us to the importance of what was happening to him during this moment of epiphany.

Hannay had got lost in the function and operation of certain tasks; they had, unseen by him, become the focus of life and as such life seemed to have little depth or great significance. 'Being' had been lost in a discipline of 'Doing'. What not only revitalised him, but gave him a new life was the sensing of what was undergirding his actions. It wasn't just a seeing of a 'big picture'; this could have been equally superficial. What was needed was depth; an understanding of 'Why?' When he grasped this, he had vision and understanding, he was ready for action and sacrifice; he had found something for which to live and die. He was a man at peace in the midst of war.

Why this is important for us is that, we too, like Hannay, far too easily get lost in function and operation; we end up in the fog of doing for its own sake. So, the temptation for us, when we look at a fresh expression of church, is to first ask questions such as, 'What are you doing?', 'What have you found that works?', 'Would you do anything differently?', 'What would you advise us to do?'. It's not that these questions are unimportant; they are important, but they are not foundational. If we make them foundational, we will lose our way and eventually become tired and disillusioned.

That's why in this section, as we focus, in particular, on the stories of eight fresh expressions of church (or potential expressions of church), we begin by asking a different set of questions. The responses to these questions then allow us to look healthily at strategy, actions and specific practice. In Part 1, we highlighted the centrality of relationship in understanding who we are as church and we noted a pressure within our society to focus on technique and results; our questions are founded on the former and resist the latter.

When talking with folk from these eight fresh expressions of church, the first question I asked was, 'What have you learnt about God?'; the second was, 'What have you learnt about yourselves as individuals and as a church community?'; and the third was, 'What have you learnt about the wider community?' The conversations around these questions weren't theoretical; they weren't the recital of catechism or the rehearsal of systematic theology. They were deeply personal and lived out and as such gave sense to the actions of these groups.

Some of the groups we have already met – Gateways in the Borders, NYNO in Aberdeen and Hot Chocolate in Dundee – the others we'll introduce as we go along. Suffice to say, they represent a wide demographic and geographical range across Scotland.

Notes

1 Buchan, John, *Mr Standfast* (1919) in *The Complete Richard Hannay Stories* (Ware: Wordsworth Classics, 2010), pp. 313–14.
2 Ibid., p. 314.

2

What Have We Learnt About God?

'The Outer Hebrides' – words that conjure contrasting images and emotions – a land at the edge or a centre of culture; wild sea shattering stone or turquoise waters washed on white sand; mist dancing through ancient circles or rain blown horizontal; mystery, intrigue and adventure or dull, introspective conservatism; Peter May intrigues or Viking lordship . . . the list could go on for a long time. Whatever our experience or preconceptions, let's journey there and meet some remarkable people in the port of Stornoway.

At the turn of the millennium, Martin's Memorial church was in a vulnerable place: its viability as an independent parish was in significant doubt; then things changed. Through an uncompromising openness to the Spirit of God and the guidance of wise and courageous leadership, the church community deepened in love and grew in number. The inherited expression of church was revitalised, and the meeting space was renovated to express this new dynamism. But the heart of God had gripped this community; Tommy MacNeil, the parish minister, puts it this way:

As we looked within our church, we saw much to encourage us and to be thankful for; a growing congregation, welcoming new people regularly, thriving children's and youth work – the list went on and on. However, when we looked at our community and asked God to show us what he saw, it was at best challenging, and at worst it was devastating. Family breakdown, poverty, addiction, mental health issues, self-harm, long term unemployment, and again, the list could go on and on.

What could we do? We reminded ourselves that God doesn't just so love the church, He so loved the world! With that truth in our hearts we began to ask God for ways in which we could best love and serve our community.[1]

This profound experience of the love of God for all led the community of Martin's Memorial to develop The Shed: a community space, where among other things, new expressions of church have evolved. The reality of being loved by God and the subsequent enthusiasm to live this out in service is at the heart of who they are and of all that they do. Speak to Tommy and he'll wax lyrical about how deep God's love and compassion is for people; how each single person is made in God's image and the value that is theirs. He'll also speak movingly of how they encounter something of God in each person whom they meet and the mutual gift that each is to the other.

One man at The Well – a Shed community of men who have alcohol and drug addiction problems – talked about being overwhelmed by the love of God. This love he experienced through other people. Once, he said, the theme of his life had been well captured in the title of an old Black Sabbath song – 'Killing Yourself to Live' – now it was just the opposite. He and others in the group were free to be themselves and not burdened by pretence.

This emphasis on the extravagant love of God, both as experience and motivation, comes across again and again in the lives of fresh expressions of church. In a town that can bring together the spirit of Johnnie Walker and the antibiotic of Alexander Fleming, rests the community of New Farm Loch, a housing scheme developed by the Council of Kilmarnock in the 1960s. St Kentigern's church has been a part of this community and has served it from its early days. In 2015, they were moved to find new ways to serve their community and be church in it; earlier they had established a 'Messy Church', and now they began to experiment with four other potential fresh expressions of church. They knew that not all of these would necessarily develop into new expressions of church community, but they had to try. Their motivation to do this was simply love. As with Martin's Memorial, they knew that they are loved and they could not help but share this, and this is evident when they gather:

> The love that God has for people is evident in the Messy Church team.

> As Messy Church, every time we meet, what comes through is that Jesus loves you – as an individual you are loved and you are precious.[2]

The intimate and foundational link between the experience and security of being loved and the capacity and desire to love is a shared refrain in the song of fresh expressions of church. The recognition of this is crucial, and it goes to the heart of our motivation for mission. When a church or a denomination is under pressure, be it due to falling numbers, ageing demographic or financial shortfall, the temptation is to 'recruit' in order to rescue or conserve what we have; the focus is on us. If this remains the aim of our reaching out, then, even if there is initial success, in the long term we will rightly fail. Crises may be the spur for considering new initiatives, but they can never be the rationale; they may be the nightmares that shatter our slumber, but they are not the vision of our waking hours. The experience of Gateways illustrates this move from initial catalyst to wholesome motivation.

> Not wanting to be negative, but an element of dissatisfaction with what was and (a sense) that there must be another way. What there is doesn't seem to be working. Looking at our area and wanting to connect with, in a way, what was real; wanting to be part of the community. Getting alongside people, seeing their needs and what they feel about the community. Got to get to know people and where they are at . . . [we were] sick of slick, professional church[3] we wanted to be authentic.

> God's love makes you want to care and pray for other people, even if the cycle of our own lives affects what we can do at any one time.

People genuinely care with a love that goes beyond human love; it is God's family, very special, I mean that with my whole heart.[4]

Linked to this is the need to recognise how easily we can be caught between paralysing fears: the fear of terminal decline and subsequent loss, the fear of risk and potential failure, the fear of success and disturbing change. These fears share a focus on self and a backing away from love. Tragically, as we back away from the radical love of God for all, we and others lose out: decline and death come to both. Love is the starting point and this, from our understanding of God as Trinity, is what we would expect.

One of the streets with the highest footfall in Scotland is Glasgow's Buchanan Street. Smack in the middle of its pedestrian pathway is St George's Tron, a church with listed structure and radically reconfigured interior. Through Art and Café, friendship and partnership it embraces the city with warmth and hospitality as it expresses being church in new and dynamic ways. For the community of St George's Tron, there is a profound sense of grace and love: 'We have learnt about God's compassion, dare we even say bias, towards the poor and marginalised.'[5]

This awareness of the overwhelming compassion of God is, in turn, shown in inclusive welcome, genuine hospitality, acts of kindness and a realising of the true dignity and worth of each person. This connection of welcome, hospitality and openness is also foundational to the life of The Well in Stornoway; one man commented enthusiastically on 'The importance of hospitality and openness to new people, who then easily feel welcome and at home'.[6]

It is impossible to emphasise enough how central this experience and subsequent motivation of love is. As we have already said, not only is it at the core of reality, but across Scotland (and I'd suspect worldwide) it is at the heart of fresh expressions of church, and rightly so, for there can be no other way forward. True, all churches should share this heart, but one of the characteristics of the eight fresh expressions of church, where I interviewed folk, was a raw, visceral awareness and experience of this love.

This embodied love was changing people; not only those who had initiated the expression of church, but those who were being loved by them. Those from the various communities and expressions of church that have developed in The Shed, in Stornoway, spoke of this again and again . . .

In their youth work, 'We have learnt about his [God's] love for the young people and how this meets young people from a variety of backgrounds and that we can show that love of God, not just in word, but in actions to all irrespective of where each young person is coming from. Young people are responding to this love . . . [they] are experiencing God's love and being overwhelmed.'[7]

In their life as a church community in all its expressions, 'The main goal is to love . . . and the communication of God's love and the first stage is to help folk learn what it is to love again. All work is under the banner of no strings attached . . . We give to others without paybacks; we express love without an agenda.'[8]

At The Well, folk emphasised the patience of God's love and the change he was making in them. The experience of love was like light that allowed them to experience forgiveness. In turn, this forgiveness freed them from fear and allowed them to be their true selves. The poison had been drawn and now they too could love and forgive. This forgiving and wanting the best for others was not necessarily easy; these men were honest about the hurt they had caused and the hurt that they had received. One man, who had forgiven a murderer, knew that had he not forgiven and shown love he would have spiralled into destruction.

The doctor and social commentator Theodore Dalrymple, in his essay, 'How – and how not – to love mankind', contrasts two nineteenth-century contemporary writers: Karl Marx and Ivan Turgenev.

Turgenev saw human beings as individuals always endowed with consciousness, character, feelings and moral strengths and weaknesses; Marx saw them always as snowflakes in an avalanche. Where Turgenev saw men, Marx saw classes of men; where Turgenev saw people, Marx saw People. These two ways of looking at the world persist into our own time and profoundly affect, for better or for worse, the solutions we propose to our social problems.[9]

Even if Dalrymple's assessment is broadstroke, it causes us to stop and think about what we mean when we say God loves *people* (not just *People*) and that we love people.

The potential emptiness of an abstraction that would love People before people was highlighted by Jean-Paul Sartre in *Nausea*, where the central character, Antoine Roquentin, challenges another's humanism by declaring that in spite of his companion's claim to love humanity he loves no-one, he only loves aspects of humanity. 'You see you don't love them . . . They are only symbols in your eyes. You aren't the least bit touched by them: you're only touched by the Youth of Man, by the Love of Man and Woman, by the Human Voice.'[10]

He put it even more strongly when he wrote, 'Evil is the systematic substitution of the abstract for the concrete.'[11]

In God's love, both the expansiveness of community and the particular of the individual are embraced; neither is sacrificed. We, on the other hand, are tempted to focus on one or the other and hence sidestep the complexity of reality and the practicalities of our responsibility.

People must never become projects; they must, in some way, always be those with whom we relate as a person to person or persons. In their book *The New Parish*, Sparks, Soerens and Friesen have a section headed, 'Misplaced love – clinging to our vision over loving people in the present'.[12] They underscore the risk of loving our vision more than loving people and love, in turn, being reduced to a technique. This is a sober challenge; with the best will and heart in the world it is easy to lose perspective.

Not surprisingly, from the nature of the initiative, fresh expressions of church have a deep awareness of mission being God's mission not ours; we are given the gift and privilege of sharing in it.

It's not our mission, but God's; God is already out there in the community and in the midst of society. Our job, our challenge, is to get alongside God and join in what he is already doing: be in the midst of life and show God's love. That's what Jesus did: he went out among people and he loved them.[13]

God is ahead and there is much more than [we] realise.[14]

This awareness of the creativity of God's Spirit, in mission, in the wider community, has, for many, been a releasing epiphany. What comes across is that, often, this realisation was not due to theological reflection, which led to the expectation of particular experiences, but rather that certain experiences caused theological reflection. This 'encounter' and subsequent contemplation is what has deepened people's understanding of God and what it means to share in God's mission; it resonates with the pattern we saw in the life of the early church when they met in Jerusalem wanting to understand what God was doing in the gentile community. This honest reflection on the complexity of their experience changed the first-century church, and the same is changing church communities today.

God's picture is bigger than ours – it is God's vision, which we share in. God is in everything and his action is much wider than we think or expect. While avoiding a universalism God is in places and situations that we would have never seen in our classic church situation. If we are listening we begin to see this.[15]

Equidistant from Edinburgh and Glasgow, the central lowlands town of Falkirk was once at the centre of Scotland's industrial revolution. The region no longer has this role, but now, among many other initiatives, it is at the centre of a web of relationships that stretches not only across Scotland, but reaches worldwide. 'Sanctuary First' is a pioneer ministry being developed by the Church of Scotland through Falkirk Presbytery.

The concept was originally developed out of the congregation of St Andrew's Parish Bo'ness, but has transitioned into what might be described as a fresh expression of church under the direct governance of Falkirk Presbytery. Albert Bogle was appointed in April 2016, as minister of Sanctuary First with the aspiration that Sanctuary First will become a worshipping congregation of the Church of Scotland on the internet . . . (Sanctuary First is) very keen to develop an authentic caring worshipping community online.[16]

We'll look in more detail later at the particular dynamic of Sanctuary First, but their experience reflects this deep awareness of God's creative activity in communities.

> God is at work in creation and in everyone's life; He is intrinsically with people . . . people pray to and worship God outside of church . . . Those outside of church think about God in a special way . . . A more inclusive attitude allows people to open up and speak about God; this allows participation [in] and development of spiritual journey.[17]

In one of his most famous poems, Gerard Manley Hopkins gives glory to the wild and free creativity of God:

> Glory be to God for dappled things . . . All things counter, original, spare, strange.[18]

But he doesn't just celebrate this as seen in nature; he celebrates it as seen in the everydayness of life:

> And all trades, their gear and tackle and trim.[19]

This wildness and creativity of God in the ordinariness of life is recognised by people as they 'listen'; and with this, to slightly misquote the famous line from *Spiderman*, comes a great freedom and a great responsibility.[20]

> [The realisation of] the creativity of God and the implications of this and of God's innovative nature for us: our understanding and our actions . . . we don't always operate in the freedom which God gives . . . [God] is innovative compared to our desire for the safe and the tried: the familiar.[21]

God who is creative and innovative is also a God of surprises. In the island and coastal parishes of Netherlorn, in Argyll, this is their experience as they experiment with forms of fresh expressions of church. Ken Ross, the parish minister, speaks of 'God being a God of surprises . . . God moments . . . which are not our activity, but are of the Spirit of the God of grace who is among us'.[22]

This experience of fresh expressions of church in Scotland and beyond integrates into a high-profile theological discussion of the second half of the twentieth and early twenty-first century: 'Missio Dei' (the mission of God) and how this relates to the being of God and nature of the church. Just as experience must not be shoehorned to fit ossified systems of theology, neither must theology be forced into serving the vagaries of casual or preferred perception. As we learn from and follow the example of the early church, the experience of fresh expressions of church informs this important theological conversation.[23]

While not always expressed in theological detail, the default intuition of many of the groups I meet is that the love of God is central in their experience and in their motivation; God's focus is on relationship and life, our challenge and privilege is how, with integrity, we, in a natural way, live this out. The reduction and abstraction of love to technique or operation is 'the kiss of death'.

There is also a sense that it isn't that God merely initiates mission or owns it. It even goes deeper than perceiving him as creating it; there seems to be an unarticulated assumption that mission is intimately a part of who God is. Mission is of God and as such God has a profound and unique relationship to it.

Mission is relational at core, and God doesn't just invite us to share in its operational aspects; that is too superficial. But, because of who we are in our being, it's deeper, more profound and urgent than this. God calls us to share in its life. Further, as mission is sensed as intimately integrated into creation as a whole and as God is understood as being active in all of his creation, then to think of God leading in mission as a co-explorer is inaccurate. The experience of fresh expressions of church is of God leading as the guide who owns, knows and loves every square nanometre of the land into which we step. There is a strong resonance with the origin of the garden in Genesis 2 and humanity's place in it.

This intimacy of God, creation, mission, call and relationship was repeatedly expressed as groups recounted God being experienced and known as the one who was in the detail, the personal and the operational, and the one who could be trusted to provide, moment by moment, in a way that was life affirming and not merely bureaucratic.

God is amongst us and [we are] trusting God to be amongst us.[24]

God has blessed abundantly, not just [in] big things, but in the detail. Folk have come to experience God's faithfulness.[25]

The importance of seeing God in small things.[26]

At times things have seemed impossible or very difficult, but God has given the capacity, gifts, ability, strength, confidence and answers to meet [these] challenges . . . God has blessed and provided practical and financial needs . . . We need to be open to the prompting of God.[27]

Have confidence that God can fulfil the vision He has given us and that He will provide gifts and skills.[28]

Trust in God with the idea he has planted – he will develop it, even if it is unclear and daunting to us . . . God is patient, faithful and he challenges us . . . Take a risk – believe that God is calling you to take it and that he will follow through . . . Have a go.[29]

There is a need to relax from an undue sense of our own responsibility, a need 'to be' in being faithful and in trusting in who we know God 'to be' . . . A need to shift from striving to go deeper in trust and to walk by faith and not by sight.[30]

As a child, I read every *Biggles* book I could find (I confess that I still read them). Biggles the hero always knew what to do, and I remember in one story,[31] when Ginger, one of Biggles's team, was separated from the group and had a difficult decision to make he asked himself, 'What would Biggles do?' This is not unlike the WWJD wristbands that were once popular.[32] To think what Jesus might do in any given situation is helpful, but there is an important distinction to be made. Fresh expression church communities are very aware of this: we are in God's image, but we are not God, so what does this mean for how we live? We radiate God's love, but God is unique in his love. Just as Trinity and incarnation are central to our life and we radiate them in our living, so too is the case with mission, but God is unique in all three.

This means that God's call to us to live mission will lead to a life, which while consonant with his being and experience will also be significantly different. So, for example, when we go and immerse ourselves in a new context and listen, serve in love and build community, we will develop a co-ownership which has an equality that is different from our relationship with God as we share in his mission.

> [The] focus is on listening and developing co-ownership . . . on being service/user led . . . The first step for The Shed is always to listen e.g. listening to folks in the community led to co-ownership in services provided; from being seen as not relevant by local statutory bodies [to] now [being] seen as instrumental in delivering their aims.[33]

This equality, which many fresh expressions of church seek with others, is not an equality we can have with God. This means we need to ponder how our being and living may totally radiate the image of God in a particular context, but not be as God wholly is in that context. Reflecting on this will help us keep focused on how we understand life, gospel and the kingdom of God.

Many issues will be raised through this reflection, including the complexity of the dynamic of equality, co-ownership and sharing the gospel of the kingdom of God. Are some groups, including fresh expressions of church, making assumptions that do not do justice to the complex intricacies of this dynamic? We will touch upon some aspects of this when we look at what fresh expressions of church have learnt about themselves and community,[34] but before this one other thought:

Just smile and wave, boys, smile and wave.[35]

So, in the film *Madagascar*, Skipper advised his band of escaping penguins, when their plan hit a problem. 'Remember, cute and cuddly, boys; Cute and cuddly', being his other advice to cause distraction.

Many times, what those in fresh expressions of church are learning about God is in a context that will not make them want to smile and wave; God is not cuddly and cute, and neither are they called to be. The churches I met were honest about this: often, because of their experience they have questions, some of which, at this moment, are not resolvable. This was most clearly expressed by NYNO (Neither Young Nor Old) as, given the demographic of their community, serious illness and death were in the warp and woof of their ongoing experience. 'God, at times, seems inscrutable . . . the ideal challenges experience and vice versa. There is no room for superficial triumphalism.'[36]

It may seem a cliché, but Jesus does call us to adventure. However, we know that stories of adventure record cost as well as exhilaration and joy. In 1743, four Russian walrus hunters were shipwrecked for over six years on the island of Edgeøya, one of the most northerly arctic landscapes on earth. Edgeøya is the third largest island of the Svalbard Archipelago and, unlike the western fjords of the largest island Spitsbergen, it doesn't benefit from the warmth of the Gulf Stream. It is hounded by gales and packs of crushing ice. When David Roberts recorded and reflected on their story,[37] he contrasted their experience with the fictions of Defoe and Wyss.[38] The latter he sees as painting a somewhat idealised fantasy, where the resourcefulness of the European, '. . . can impose a western order upon the chaos of the wilderness'.[39] In contrast, he writes that the reality of the stranded walrus hunters' lives was much darker; nature would not be domesticated or conquered, it only brokered being listened to and heeded: '. . . on Edgeøya nature rules with implacable severity and the sailors survive by fitting their lives to its demands'.[40]

Roberts challenges the cheap search for moral or meaning imposed upon this story, be this via the rational optimism of the Enlightenment or the instructive lessons of children's tales.[41]

Survival stories, in general, promise to tell us something basic about the human condition. From them, we earnestly attempt to wring some insight 'into the meaning of life'. And bad movies and potboiler novels only too willingly oblige, offering trite upbeat formulas by which their protagonists vow to live out the rest of their days, or supplying saccharine evidence that God will answer our prayers in the darkest of predicaments.

It is the need to believe that suffering has a transcendent meaning that has turned Anne Frank's complex *The Diary of a Young Girl*, with its precocious meditations on evil, its exploration of her own budding sexuality, into the homiletic melodrama of its stage adaption, reduced to a pious fantasia on her most famous line, 'in spite of everything I still believe that people are really good at heart'.[42]

Roberts's observation and challenge is important for us, not because there is no love and sense to reality, but because this will only be experienced, by us and others, if we face the complexity of what really is 'head on' and acknowledge that we may never fully understand 'Why?'. Aslan is not safe, but he is good.

The other helpful reminder from Roberts's contrast of the fantasy desert islands and the brutally real arctic one is how we engage with our context. For the solitary and the family in Defoe's and Wyss's tales they could impose their way on their new environment, the walrus hunters couldn't. The latter had to listen and let their life be shaped by that which surrounded them. However, this realistic humility was not a defeat or a denial of what they wanted to achieve: survival – three of them lived to tell the tale. So too, even in the harshest conditions of cultural pressure, where meaning feels lost, we listen and are shaped, but not in a way that denies either who we are or what is in our heart. We are humble, but not humiliated; shaped, but in being so we shape from within that which surrounds us.

Notes

1 Tommy MacNeil, see article in Part 3.

2 St Kentigern's interview.

3 It was not being implied that the traditional or inherited expression of church, in the local parish, was 'slick and professional'. This was a general comment that slick (technique) professionalism lacked the genuineness and depth which they were seeking; it was not the model or ethos that they should adopt if they were to engage with their community in open, loving, serving mission.

4 Gateways interview.

5 St George's Tron interview.

6 The Shed interview.

7 The Shed interview.

8 Martin's Memorial interview.

9 Dalrymple, Theodore, *Our Culture, What's Left of It: The Mandarins and the Masses* (Chicago: Ivan R. Dee, 2005), p. 77.

10 Sartre, Jean-Paul, *Nausea* (Harmondsworth: Penguin, 1976 [1938]), p. 172.

11 'St. Genet: Actor and Martyr', quoted in Sparks, Paul, Soerens, Tim and Friesen, Dwight J., *The New Parish: How Neighborhood Churches Are Transforming Mission, Discipleship and Community* (Downers Grove, IL: IVP, 2014), p. 67.

12 Sparks, Soerens and Friesen, *The New Parish*, pp. 69–72.

13 St Kentigern's interview.

14 Shed youth worker interview.

15 Gateways interview.

16 Sanctuary First website www.sanctuaryfirst.org.uk.

17 Interview with Albert Bogle.

18 Hopkins, Gerard Manley, 'Pied Beauty', 1918.

19 Hopkins, 'Pied Beauty', 1918.

20 'With great power comes great responsibility', Uncle Ben's words to Peter Parker (Spiderman) as he begins to come to terms with his new abilities. Though in the original story (*Amazing Fantasy*, 15 August 1962) Uncle Ben did not say these words; only in later accounts of the 'origin story' were they attributed to him. In the original, after Uncle Ben's murder, the narrator ends the story by commenting, 'And a lean, silent figure slowly fades into the gathering darkness, aware at last that in this world, with great power must also come great responsibility'. It has been pointed out to me that others significantly preceded Stan Lee, e.g. William Lamb MP, 'that the possession of great power necessarily implies great responsibility' (House of Commons, Habeas Corpus Suspension Bill, Hansard, 27 June 1817, Vol. 36, c.1227). Also, these words reflect Jesus' teaching (Matthew 25:14–30) on using responsibly that we have been given; passivity is not an option in the parable of the talents.

21 Interview with Alastair Duncan, St George's Tron, Glasgow.

22 Interview with Ken Ross, Netherlorn churches.

23 See for example, Moynagh, Michael, *Church for Every Context: An Introduction to Theology and Practice* (Norwich: SCM Press, 2013), pp. 120–34; Lings, *Reproducing Churches*, pp. 73–93.

24 Hot Chocolate interview.

25 The Shed (Murdo) interview.

26 NYNO interview.

27 St Kentigern's interview.

28 Gateways interview.

29 St Kentigern's interview.

30 St George's Tron interview.

31 I can't remember which story as it was a long time ago, also the scenario reflected a general premise regarding Biggles's authority, ability and leadership.

32 WWJD: What Would Jesus Do?

33 The Shed interview.

34 Some of our discussion on discipleship in Part 3 will also relate to this.

35 *Madagascar*, DreamWorks, 2005.

36 NYNO (Neither Young Nor Old) interview.

37 Roberts, David, *Shipwrecked on the Top of the World: Four Against the Arctic* (London: Simon and Schuster, 2003). References from the Little, Brown 2004 edition.

38 Defoe, Daniel, *Robinson Crusoe* (1719) and Wyss, Johann, *The Swiss Family Robinson* (1812).

39 Roberts, *Shipwrecked on the Top of the World*, p. 284.

40 Roberts, *Shipwrecked on the Top of the World*, p. 284.

41 Roberts, *Shipwrecked on the Top of the World*, p. 284.

42 Roberts, *Shipwrecked on the Top of the World*, p. 285.

3

What Have We Learnt
About Ourselves?

War is brutal, and atrocity is part of its hellish landscape; it offers death to every part of our nature. Civil war intensifies the darkness, the bitterness and the ulcerating wound. In *The Outlaw Josey Wales*,[1] a film set during the American Civil War, the title character's family are brutally murdered by Union-supporting 'Red Leg' paramilitaries. Wales, who until this point has been a peaceful farmer, an innocent to violence, is reduced to a shell of a man. Driven by a thirst for vengeance, he joins a Confederate guerrilla band.

At the end of the war most of his group surrender, but they are massacred on their laying down of arms. Wales kills some of the soldiers responsible, ending up a wanted man, hounded with a bounty on his head. Pursued, he finds a certain solace in solitude, 'I don't want nobody to belong to me'. A little later, we see that this sentiment is in part due to the fear of losing those who come close to him. His words, 'Everyone I like doesn't seem to stick around long', reflect his experience that most whom he has loved or cared for have died violently. However, as he travels, he meets different characters, characters who are portrayed as either misfits or vulnerable and abused. Initially, he steps back from them, but their lives become intertwined with his; they become his new family, and while he may bring them acceptance and protection, they offer him a form of redemption. We sense that with and through them he finds life, love and eventually himself, something that would not have happened in the loneliness of isolation.

This outworking of the life of Josey Wales shouldn't surprise us; like so much, it resonates with our understanding of the Trinity. So, our being made in God's image means that isolation is not a wholesome option. But the end of Josey Wales's story mustn't blind us to how the loss, the emptiness and the process of redemption also mirror much of our life both as individuals and as church. Though relatively few of us in the West have experienced the trauma of the book and film's hero (though this sadly is not true for many people in other parts of our world), we do need, as church communities, to face up to our particular loss, grief and anger, and to what this has done, or threatens to do, to us. We also need to embrace others who are very different from us, if we are to, not only love and serve them, but also become more and more our true and 'whole' selves.

This openness can be deeply unsettling and requires a profound honesty, but for church communities it has been crucial as they have considered developing fresh expressions of church.

God uses our previous experiences, even the difficult ones.[2]

Being authentic, transparent and being real is key.[3]

Need to be open to God . . . we have learnt to be open to change. This has changed us and deepened our understanding of what it is to be church.[4]

A vulnerable openness to be honest and to the consequences of this honesty has been essential for individuals and groups to better understand who they are. This honesty often grows as they appreciate more and more who God is; they experience a freedom and, in time, a joy. Fear in its various avatars, including, as with Josey Wales, the fear of loving and losing, begins to fade.

Further, this relating to others, in the experience of those fresh expressions I interviewed, is often the way in which faith, understanding and an awareness of God has deepened and developed. They recognise that they have prospered by being together as a community which serves God and others; theoretical knowledge alone could not have brought about this change for good.

[We are] convinced that this 'living out together' is not just the best way to do mission, but inimitable to God's presence among us.[5]

Church is not dependent on one person's vision and action, but on the church community and each person using their gifts and opportunities. The church is not the Minister, it is the people and they are responsible for mission . . . the importance of mutual support and prayer within the group.[6]

The mutual responsibility to remind one another . . .[7]

This importance of community was also reflected in what groups thought about leadership. Although pioneers, they were not wanting to be 'Lone Rangers':

There is a need for a leadership team, or at least one other leader to explore imaginatively the way forward. The process of change is stressful for the leader and the community; a team helpfully changes the dynamic.[8]

The Netherlorn group of churches emphasised that our development of relationships should not be restricted to a local context, but should include relating to churches and communities overseas. For them, these wider relationships had reaped a rich harvest for both the inherited and fresh expressions of church as well as for the wider community, benefiting integration of church and community.

For love, care and growth to develop to their full potential, groups were intentional about ensuring that relationships had the best opportunity to blossom and not remain superficial. There was no contentment with a mere appearance of welcome, hospitality and companionship.

[There is] the need to get to know one another as there is not a shared history; this is an on-going challenge, not just for those who have been there from the beginning, but as new people link with the community. The Café Church dynamic, with the focus on hospitality and food helps the development of this dynamic.

Even after five years we are still at the forming stage, 'we don't know one another at the level where it matters'. This reflects the need of having to 'go wide' in the first stage in order to make lots of relationships [community and individuals]; it takes time to really deepen relationships. Now is the time to 'go deeper' with church community and the church community recognises this.[9]

It's important to pause here and recognise that churches that have initiated fresh expressions of church and fresh expressions of church themselves embrace fragility, not in a pitiful, 'Woe is me', sense, but in the sense of freedom to live. This may seem counter-intuitive, but in reality it is the 'natural' and appropriate way to live. To attempt to incubate or foster independence, of God or other people, is a futile folly of pride which paves the way to destruction. Our individualistic Western culture may promote this delusion, as may our self-centredness, but it is a temptation to be robustly resisted. Groups recognise that this interdependence is, in some ways, countercultural for many whom they meet – even if deep down it is what they desire: 'People are more "privatised". There is less sense of community, people are more home and TV focused and they have less contact with neighbours . . . older people have a memory of community, younger folk don't . . . we need to identify or create points where people can meet.'[10]

It is no surprise that in this context of trust and relationship, where fragility is openly owned, prayer was emphasised as core to the life of these groups. This was highlighted by St Kentigern's; they were conscious of growing in the sharing and in the leading of prayer. My impression was that prayer had become a much more natural action for them as a group. They were not alone in this; in Stornoway, the youth leaders at The Shed underscored the centrality of prayer and how it was their first reaction to a situation. Group and individual prayer was intentional and focused, as 'Prayer realigns and helps the focus to be on God, which is the main thing . . . Leaders have a deep hunger for God, which fires their hunger for the young people to have this deep hunger: a personal, passionate pursuit of God'.[11]

This brings us to motivation, which was something that both the churches that initiated fresh expressions of church and the ensuing innovations were very honest about. 'We need to be honest about what we are doing and why. We can fool ourselves and think we are doing something for God, but in reality it is for us: our control and power.'[12]

In Ezekiel (chapter 28) there is a picture of evil forming in the heart of the king of Tyre. This evil comes from a focus on and enchantment with self; pride and self-centredness seduce him to claim personal divinity and to demand the thrall of others. There is a stark warning for us here, for the king of Tyre is not alone: his vanity is also ours. We may not consciously set ourselves up as divine, but if we work to shape the world (immediate and, through our governments, global) to our will and comfort, then, in practice, we are setting ourselves up as gods, albeit petty ones.

The chapter in Ezekiel echoes images from the garden in Genesis 2 and 3 and as such beckons us to recognise how universal is this weakness and motivation. The fresh expressions of church which I spoke to are very aware of this temptation, both for them and for the churches which initiated them. Falling numbers, failing finance and the decay of treasured buildings threaten that which not only gives comfort, but to a significant degree can anchor identity. But, as we said earlier, while these may cause us distress, they cannot be what motivate us to share the life which Jesus offers. Should this be so, then we are trying to place the gospel of Christ at our service, to suit our needs. Harsh as it may seem, we are in fact trying to be lord over Jesus and bring about, not the Father's kingdom, but ours. We have all done this, so none of us can point a finger. '[There must be] no personal gain in motivation.'[13]

Commenting on Acts 1:6–8, Tom Wright contrasts our desire for authority, which belongs to God alone, with the power which he gives us through his authority:

God has authority, and it is through him and from him that all authorised rule in the world must flow. We don't have that ultimate authority: no human in whatever task or role ever does. It all comes from God. But what God's people are promised is power; the word used here is *dynamis* from which we get the word dynamite. We need that power just as Jesus' first followers did if we are to be his witnesses, to find ways of announcing to the world that he is already rightful king and lord.[14]

This contrast was highlighted by a leader in Hot Chocolate, and as we will see later is significantly influential in their approach to discipleship.

Authority is the capacity to set and know i.e. the authority to control. We can see why the disciples wanted to be in on this. The power, which the disciples are given, is not control, but to be enabled to be in the world and be witnesses: power to live in the world, power to declare Christ, but not [to have] the authority of the Father. In church we spend a lot of time acting as though we have, or should have, authority, but that we don't have the power to do anything. Jesus is saying the reverse. We need to go out with confidence and move with the God-given power of the Holy Spirit – not the power to control or order the life of another, but to share the life [of Christ] and love them; power to listen to the pain and not be overwhelmed, power to rejoice with them and not be jealous.[15]

Our companion fresh expressions of church are understanding more and more who they are as they experience and understand more who God is. There is an intrinsic, as well as an intentional, reflective living. There is a growing peace and rest which is lived out in confident love and service (not on a slumbering 'on laurels'). There is openness to radical change and a moving away from fear. They are not perfect, but they are making a difference . . . and rightly they celebrate this.

This last point of celebration is important, for it would be easy for a false humility or stoicism to set in. Dante in his *Divine Comedy* observes that, as he approaches Paradise, there flows a spring which divides in two: one stream represents an acknowledgement of the wrong one has done and the other represents an acknowledgement of the good. His guide tells him that it is essential to taste both waters.[16] This mutual acknowledgement is important if we are to face up to the complexity and reality of life, and to the grace of God. Fresh expressions of church experience both the anguish and the exuberance of life; they are open to shame and honour, but are self-seeking in neither.

Earlier we underscored the centrality of church being based on relationships, from which practices develop, not vice versa. For some whom I interviewed, this was initially quite challenging, as so much of their previous experience of church and their identity as Christians had related to certain actions – actions that the church community and culture assumed not only as normative, but intrinsic to being a member of the church.

So, taking away that doing church bit and then seeing what's left was quite challenging: what if this is all there is? But, it isn't really; it was quite a revelation in working out how to be a Christian . . .

There was a focus on being, on relationships: seeing what it is to be a Christian and then rebuilding an understanding and practice of being church. This new understanding, through Gateways, has not meant loss, but new ways of connecting. There was the need to avoid the false ease and comforts of old patterns and practices and take the risk . . .

There is no pressure to conform e.g. to assumptions about attendance, to be part of the community – belonging is deeper than this.[17]

This new awareness has involved not only the recognition and celebration of people's gifts, but the freedom and encouragement to develop them.

[The church] is not dependent on one person . . . but on the church community and each using their gifts, experience and opportunities.[18]

Leaders complement one another in focus, gifts and relationships.[19]

It's incredible the skills folk have and the freedom they have to develop and use them.[20]

True, this recognition and freedom should be in every expression of church, but in the fresh expressions I have met it is expected, sought out and encouraged. This is the default practice, not just a theoretical assent; it is assumed that the church will wither if this area of its community life does not blossom. In a way, this openness, expectation and clear intention is not surprising in a fresh expression of church, as one of the core assumptions is that church is not brought and transplanted into a community. Church should be indigenous to the new context and develop fully from within it and from the resources which God has given it.

> God can use anybody, not just Christians. He draws people into involvement: he puts a desire in their hearts in the first place. They want to belong, help, be involved . . . This happens a lot in Gateways: people just seem to want to help and this has a knock-on effect; so many strands grow unseen, like mushrooms . . . because of a sense of family and community, and the ownership that has developed from this everyone takes responsibility for the practicalities of the church . . . Everybody cares.[21]

Leadership, as well as involvement, is not always provided by the 'usual suspects', and this openness and recognition blooms when those, who traditionally might be seen as the leaders of any initiative, don't feel threatened or devalued by the talents, experience, vision, enthusiasm and innovation of others.

For this to happen, all need confidence and humility: a confidence and humility that come from being captivated by God's love for them and for others. In a national context where inherited church communities feel threatened and vulnerable, this is not always easy. We are tempted to look out for ourselves, we can become envious of the success of others, and with closures, unions and linkages we want to 'be the last person standing'. The experience of fresh expressions of church points us in a very different direction. However, while it may be a direction towards life, it may also necessitate the death of the seed that planted it.[22]

This brings us to the relationship between the inherited or traditional expression of church and the fresh expression which it initiated. This can be a mixed experience, often highlighted by the expectations of and reaction to Messy Church.

> Messy Church is an all-age fresh expression of church that offers counter-cultural transformation of family life through families coming together to be, to make, to eat and to celebrate God.[23]

> Messy Church isn't a way of getting people to come to church on Sunday – There are examples of people starting in Messy Church and deciding to join Sunday church as well but these are the exception rather than the rule. If people wanted to go to established church, they would be going by now. Messy Church is interdependent with established church, but will usually operate as a separate congregation or church.[24]

This clarity, which Messy Church emphasises, is essential for avoiding confusion, hurt and discouragement in the relationship between inherited and fresh expressions of church. Yet even when an inherited expression of church knows that it is initiating a fresh expression of church, there can still be a later misunderstanding. This may be because not everyone in the inherited expression of church has understood what a fresh expression of church is, or it may be because some have a narrow understanding of what church is (the community that gathers on a Sunday morning), or it might be out of self-centredness: 'Why should we invest in this gathering, when we see no return on Sundays? It's only using up limited resources of time, people and money and the church is not growing.'

This can obviously be disheartening for those who are seeing a new church community establish and grow, and it is important that there are strong advocates within the inherited expression of church for this nascent community. While those in the fresh expression of church have a responsibility to communicate their vision and share what God is doing, it is the responsibility of leaders and others in the traditional expression of church not only to stand with them (including when mistakes are made), but to shield and honour them in the face of misunderstanding or misrepresentation. When this dynamic is present, there can be freedom, warmth, mutual respect and encouragement between the complementary expressions of church.

Those in Gateways emphasise the freedom they have had in not being seen as a feed-in to the inherited expression of church in their village. 'There is a genuine partnership and fellowship with other groups. We have not conformed to pressure to be an inherited expression of church; there is a celebration of mixed economy.'[25]

Yet, even when from the beginning the particular call of a fresh expression of church has been clear, it takes grace, on the part of all, to maintain this perspective, particularly when there is a need in the traditional expression of church. For many groups, it can be difficult to find the correct balance between, on the one hand, supporting and working together, and, on the other hand, compromising their own call and mission by overinvolvement in meeting the needs of another group.

Although the pressure may seem more one-way as a fresh expression develops and factors such as ageing challenge the traditional expression, we need to remember that the traditional expression of church has also had to discern its capacity and the resources it needs to serve the community with which it is actually engaging. At some point, it has had to weigh up the implications of releasing resources to develop a new expression of church for its own ability to fulfil the particular form of mission to which God has called it.

Like all relationships, this dynamic is complex and the experience within the Church of Scotland reflects this complexity, with many of the constructive and not-so-constructive outcomes evident. The relationship between the inherited expression of church in Martin's Memorial and the fresh expressions of church in The Shed is very positive, but this is not serendipitous:

A key strength has been the intentional nature of the work of The Shed and the ongoing communication of this with the inherited expression of church. The initial and ongoing engagement of the inherited church has been core to the development of The Shed . . . The importance of communication so that the inherited church can continue to own and engage with the work of The Shed.[26]

The experience of some other churches has been different. Sometimes the groups have drifted apart and are like old friends who now rarely see each other, but hold fond memories. For some others, there has been an intentional, mutually agreed separation of identity, where good relationships are maintained and where there may be regular shared activities. In some other cases, the split has been more like an acrimonious divorce. The reasons why these outcomes develop are many, but lessons we have learnt include:

- The necessity of a continued openness to God. Without this, we work on a residual vision and enthusiasm, which in time will be eroded.
- The need to remind ourselves and one another about who we are and how we are loved by God, and then rest in the identity and security that comes from this.
- We must pray for this love to be experienced by others; we must love others, not just a vision, a community or an institution.
- Humility in all concerned. Those in the traditional church need to be open to the new, to sacrifice and to painful change. Those who are pioneering the fresh expression of church must not be arrogant or impatient; they too must be equally willing to learn.
- The need to ensure that we communicate with one another in ways that make it easy for each to understand the heart, hopes and challenges of the other.
- It is essential to listen to one another, really hear and take in what is being said and felt by the other. Even if we feel that a criticism is 99 per cent unfair, take seriously the valid 1 per cent.
- The need to be honest about our motivation.

- How easily we can become self-focused or self-centred. With great generosity, we may initially release resources, but if we become stretched, decline or lose profile in a community, due to the success of the other, then ill-feeling and jealousy readily knock at our door.
- The need to pass on vision and depth of relationship from one generation to the next. This does not just relate to age profile, but also to generations of leaders. We have mentioned a number of times that relationships are at the core of being church; as this is true in general, it is also true for leaders. At the beginning of a fresh expression initiative and as it continues, the initial generation of leaders in both expressions of church hopefully understand, support and are advocates for one another. However, when a change of leadership takes place in either group, then the same understanding and closeness cannot be assumed; this change has to be prepared for and relationships have to be intentionally formed and deepened.
- A church that is innovative in its expression, or even is a fresh expression of church, cannot be assumed to understand the context of a new expression of church that may emerge from mission in a fresh setting. In fact, because it is in itself innovative, it may assume that it is at the cutting edge of mission for all contexts. This may be a significant stumbling block, as it takes a particular humility to recognise one's new position in a changing cultural world (a little like the moment when someone finds that the pop music of their youth is now on Radio 2).

In Part 3, we'll think more about the relationship between inherited and fresh expressions of church, but for now let's conclude with some music.

When leaders from St George's Tron were asked the question, 'What theme song or anthem would you choose for your church?', there were different ideas, but the one which sparked most discussion was 'Take Five', by Dave Brubeck. In fact, it wasn't so much the piece of music that was important, but the style of improvised jazz. At the core of this type of music, there is something basic, which can be imaginatively developed. Yet before there can be any improvising, this basic core has to be understood.

In turn, the improvisation is not merely random. It demands both a discipline and a freedom. To improvise well, each musician has to listen with respect to the other musicians; each player has value and each actively contributes to the whole. The process is intrinsically organic and unpredictable, but it is not chaotic; it is a triumphant expression of life, energy and significant joy.

Not a bad way to think about a fresh expression of church.

Notes

1 *The Outlaw Josey Wales*, directed by Clint Eastwood, Warner Bros, 1976; based on Carter Forrest, *The Rebel Outlaw: Josey Wales* (Whipporwill Publishers, 1972) republished in 1975 under the title *Gone to Texas*.

2 Gateways.

3 Gateways.

4 St Kentigern's.

5 Hot Chocolate interview.

6 St Kentigern's interview.

7 Netherlorn interview.

8 NYNO interview.

9 St George's Tron interview.

10 St Kentigern's interview.

11 The Shed interview.

12 Hot Chocolate interview.

13 Hot Chocolate interview.

14 Wright, Tom, *Acts for Everyone* (London: SPCK, 2008), pp. 6–9 (9), commenting on Acts 1:6–8.

15 Hot Chocolate interview.

16 Dante, *Divine Comedy*, translated by Allen Mandelbaum (London: Everyman's Library, 1995), *Purgatorio* Canto 28, lines 121–33, p. 349.

17 Gateways interview.

18 St Kentigern's interview.

19 The Shed (youth work) interview.

20 Gateways interview.

21 Gateways interview.

22 John 12:20–3.

23 Messy Church website, www.messychurch.org.uk/. Claire Dalpra of The Sheffield Centre.

24 Messy Church website, www.messychurch.org.uk/. The false expectation that Messy Church's role is to feed into the Sunday gathering is widespread and illustrates a deep, cultural misunderstanding of church, which has been confused with a Biblical understanding.

25 Gateways interview.

26 The Shed interview.

4

What Have We Learnt About Our Community?

'All animals are equal, but some are more equal than others.'[1]

The famous line from *Animal Farm* doesn't only apply to totalitarian regimes, but causes us to ask questions about other political and social systems. So, for example, what does equality mean in a democracy? All can vote, but not all can access or process the same detail of information upon which decisions are made. Or think of the detailed terms to which we are often asked to agree when accessing products or services on the internet; has everyone equally got the time and/or the capacity to engage with this transparency?

This type of question or consideration is important when we think about the integrity of fresh expressions of church as they develop in new communities. We speak about the cultural context shaping the expression of church that evolves, and the community in some way co-owning what is developing. In reality, what is meant by this? Is there a danger that, as with Orwell's phrase, something is being presented in a way that attempts to give a better impression than is really the case?

A consistent refrain of the folk to whom I spoke was that they were not merely doing something for people; they were doing something with people. Indeed, I sensed that it went deeper than this: it wasn't that they were primarily even doing something with people; they were 'being with people' and from this 'being with', relationships then developed, which, in turn, were lived out together.

First and foremost, Hot Chocolate is not here to do things for young people. We are not here to provide a service for young people, but instead to grow a community with young people. That subtle difference actually makes all the difference . . . Since the outset, it has been the young people who have made the decisions about how, when and what happens. These roots remain totally foundational to who we are and the way we operate today . . .[2]

Hot Chocolate is particularly sensitive to how the 'making of meaning relates to power and control';[3] they consciously avoid any form of manipulation as they foster deep and honest relationships within the community. As they are working with teenagers and young adults, they are sensitive to their stage of development, their reaction to authority and their intrinsic curiosity. The latter, they note, is often undervalued in a church context.

We are still unpicking the extent to which we have, consciously or unconsciously, absorbed the dynamics of the Enlightenment and Modernism . . . The extent to which we stay in control, where people know the rules leaves the power dynamics unexposed and unexplored. For example, in exploring the Bible, if we stay in control of the message it will 'bounce back'. However, if we are prepared to explore and allow our understanding to be vulnerable to the reaction of others – apathy, scorn etc., then we have a possibility to find something that will resonate with them; something more deeply truthful and embodied – more like the discipling of Jesus and Paul . . . Control of meaning is a key technique of abusers . . . What is more important, Truth and Love, or Order and staying in Control of our Reputation; the Organisation can begin to take precedence.[4]

But what does this mean in practice; where does the initiative, the guidance, the shaping and the giving of significance really lie? The short answer is of course, 'With God', but how have fresh expressions of church and communities experienced this?

Previously, when we looked at what we have been learning about God, we pointed out that while we may radiate God's love, God is unique in his love. Trinity, incarnation and mission may be central to our life and we may reflect these in our living, but God is unique in all three. God's call to us to share in his mission will lead to a life, which while consonant with his being and experience, will also be significantly different. So when we go and immerse ourselves in a new context and listen, serve in love and build community, we can develop a co-ownership with this community; this co-ownership has an equality that can never be in our relationship with God. Our being and living may totally radiate the image of God in a particular context, but can never be as God wholly is in that context.

How then do we understand this dynamic of not being God in a context, yet being the heralds of God's kingdom; desiring an equality with others, yet allowing the church to be fully church in this new culture? How can we lead, without controlling? How, with integrity, can we shape while also being shaped? How do we avoid making assumptions that do not do justice to the complex intricacies of this dynamic?

The first point to underscore is that the churches and groups that I interviewed were not playing games; they neither wanted to fool themselves, nor others. They had a blazing integrity that came from love.

Second, all in the community that is being served, irrespective of what their faith is, simply by virtue of being part of this community, will intrinsically have a potentially active role in shaping the new ecclesial community. Their network and quality of relationships affect the quality of the life of a community. Further, at the very least, they will be listened to by those initiating the fresh expression of church. So, potentially all have some active role to play.

Third, our understanding of the incarnation helps us here. Throughout its history, the Church has declared as non-negotiable that neither divinity nor humanity was compromised in the incarnation of the Second Person of the Trinity. So, in Part 1, we emphasised that in the development of a fresh expression of church, neither the integrity of being church, nor the integrity of the community with which the church is engaging should in any way be compromised. Yet in the incarnation, divinity took the initiative and it brought both challenge and hope to the human context.

This latter point is of real, practical significance. When a church engages with a community in a fresh expression initiative, it first listens. But what does this listening entail? We will consider this in more depth in Part 3, but here we need to remember:

- The church is a herald of hope, with a unique message of love and grace. Our listening and our service must not deny either this spiritual reality or the need of the individual and the community; if we deny either, then we have compromised our integrity and jettisoned the example of the incarnation.
- Listening and engaging with people is not a clinical exercise; it is deeply relational and potentially community-building. As welcome and hospitality are core to the life of a new ecclesial community, all will be welcomed to share in the life of the community of the fresh expression of church.
- This welcome however is not at root to be a guest, but to be part of a family. Many years ago, when I first met the person who was to become my wife, I knew none of her family. Then came the day when I first met them (she comes from a big family, so it was a bit overwhelming). But it didn't stop there; from initially being a virtual stranger, receiving warm hospitality, I became more and more integrated into the life of the family. Even before my wife and I married and I became a formal member of the family, I participated in its life and I had responsibility within it. True welcome is an invitation to be a participant rather than a guest, but the progression from one to the other is normally a process.
- The fresh expressions of churches I meet understand people as 'whole' people – physical, emotional, social, intellectual and spiritual – they reject a dualism. This means that through any facet of their humanity a person can engage with the life of the church community and in doing so bring the whole of their humanity into its life. Engagement with

the church community is never a unidimensional 'spiritual' interface. Therefore, each person, through whatever form of engagement, can potentially affect the whole sphere of the church's life: social, spiritual etc.

- The wider community is not bereft of the Spirit of God, and the experience of the fresh expressions of church which I met was that they had discovered God's presence in the community. They had seen God's image reflected in many individuals and groups.

> God is at work in creation and in everyone's life; he is intrinsically with people . . . Those outside of the church think about God in a special way . . . a more inclusive attitude allows people to open up and speak about God; this allows participation in and the development of a spiritual journey . . . People are open [for you] to pray, with and for them, when they know that you are not setting yourself up as being closer to God than they are.[5]

This quotation from Sanctuary First illustrates the balance we have been thinking about. The church is not pretending to be God; it is not giving individuals within it, or the church community itself, a dignity and value which it does not attribute equally to all. It is free to take an initiative, but not impose it; just as the wider community, or anyone within it, is free to take, but not impose an initiative. But how then do we decide which initiatives to suggest and which to accept? This brings us to our next two considerations.

- What qualities of the kingdom of God are reflected in the life of a community? Here we need to look and listen well; it would be all too easy, depending on where we were coming from, to focus only on the positive or the negative. We need to relate to the whole of what is going on. Yet having said this, we will also need to focus on particular positives and negatives. The experience and reflections of The Shed are very helpful here. Their context is the very traditional culture of Lewis, one which in their experience does not easily embrace change.

There are many unhelpful ideas of church by local authorities, statutory groups and wider church . . . The approach of love, listening and co-ownership has broken pre-conceptions of church.[6]

Their approach is one that has fostered trust, honesty and transparency. It has helped people face up to what was harmful, through focusing not on the negatives, but on what they believed was deep within each person. This did not hinder them challenging one another; what it did do was provide a constructive way to engage with that which was destructive and contrary to the kingdom of God.

Some folk feel that in the midst of their mess and slipping up they have got to pretend that everything is ok. It took me to be able to say, 'Don't think you've got to hide what is going on; we will never judge you. We only want to love and support you.' Then to see the shift in their mind, 'It's ok, I can be real'. They may not feel that they are worthy of love. This needs to be worked out in their context . . .

Because of relationships with folk and the context from which they are coming there has been a focus on encouraging what is deep within them, rather than focusing on the negatives. We are challenging them in the context of what they know and what pulls them away from the negatives. Focus is not on the mess, but on drawing out from within them what they know to be true.

[We] focus on what people know deep down, not on censure; where people are today does not define them for tomorrow. This has opened folk to ask 'Why?'[7]

St Kentigern's has also found that their love for and openness to the wider community has changed how they, as a church, are perceived.

> The heart of the church to serve was recognised . . .
> people are seeing us in a different way.[8]

The honesty, transparency and trust that groups have created allow them not only to emphasise the assets found in a community and encourage those relationships and behaviours which resonate with the kingdom of God, but also to recognise where the kingdom of God brings a particular challenge.

As those who hope to initiate a fresh expression of church become increasingly integrated into a community, they identify that which denies the love of God and the life that he offers us. But because they recognise that Jesus is lord of this community, they don't step back; they love, they engage and they share how for both individual and community life can be different. But they do not do this from a place of superiority; they have created a level playing field of dignity and vulnerability. They do not try to usurp the place of Jesus, but in a setting of mutual accountability, with the wisdom and grace of the Holy Spirit, they can both challenge and affirm. Co-ownership does not necessarily imply equality of discernment.

- When a fresh expression of church asks the question, 'What particular aspects of the Good News do people in this new context need to hear?', it's tempting to answer, 'What do you mean? They need to hear it all.' However, this misunderstands the question. We are not being invited to cherry-pick through the gospel to find that which is palatable so that this can be presented and the rest binned. The question really is, 'Given the experience of this community and individuals within it, what is the first thing that God wants them to experience and understand about his love and grace?' So, for example, as we saw earlier, youth workers in The Shed emphasised that folk did not have to pretend; they could be brutally honest. God's love and their love for the young people was not conditional on the 'mess' or otherwise of their lives; first and foremost, they needed to know that they were loved, for they felt unworthy of this.

This sensitivity is not something that occurs haphazardly. It is something that develops as the groups actively listen to God and to those in the new context in which they are serving.

- As those initiating a fresh expression of church get to know their new community, not in an abstract, impersonal way, but in a deeply profound and personal way, they begin to discern how to be and how to live in this community. The challenge and comfort of kingdom and gospel lead the way and with integrity, partnerships and co-ownership develop in a variety of creative and life-giving ways.

This incredible renewal is happening in large part because people . . . have realised that there is no controlling technique, no magic code or habits of highly effective people that can take the place of practicing love, friendship and Spirit-led collaboration within the neighbourhood.[9]

There are three other lessons that groups have learnt that it would be easy to bypass, because we might take them for granted.

The first is that as communities were listened to, what was heard was not only the particularities (or peculiarities) of that community, but also the effects on that community of what was happening in the wider society and world. Effects, which in many important ways they had no hand in bringing about; for example, the consequences of the global financial crisis on communities after 2008, or the changes that advances in technology and social media drive. The challenge is to discern how these communities are affected, the nuances involved and what this means for loving service, discipleship and the evolving of a contextually sensitive fresh expression of church.

The leaders of Hot Chocolate commented on the pressure that society as a whole is putting on young people: '. . . the degree of stress and anxiety, which many young people battle with and how much of this comes from a view of self that is underpinned by economics, consumerism and a vacuous post-modernism'.[10]

They considered how this general pressure in society affects the specific community and people whom they are serving. So, for example, the message, 'you can be anything you want', is acutely damaging for young people: it opens the road to failure. No-one can be anything they want; we all have limitations, and many factors in life are beyond our control. Young people are particularly vulnerable to this distortion, as their life at this point is less defined, less under control.

Second, we learn about communities through relationship and witnessing others in relationship. Earlier we noted Sartre's criticism of abstraction and the loss of love for the individual; it is a very important point, which we mustn't lose sight of. When considering how we understand and value another person, Rowan Williams comments on how prison guards find it easier to dehumanise prisoners if they keep them isolated from those who love them. Once the guards experience that a prisoner is loved by another, it is much more difficult to ignore their humanity and refuse to relate to them as fellow humans.[11]

So too it is with the developments of fresh expressions of church. Yes, statistics must be looked at, social research may be done, and we may abstract trends and characteristics, but this should only be in the context of relating to people and experiencing how they relate one to another; only in the context of listening, of conversations, of community and of love. If relationship is not there, the results will be sterile.

There is a focus on people and relationships.[12]

Folk in church are involved in the wider community e.g. the local Community Council would have folded if it had not been for folk in church communities becoming involved and 'saving it'; this has been recognised by the Council.[13]

In his 2018 television series, *The Secrets of Cinema*, Mark Kermode chose the romantic comedy as the first genre to be considered.[14] He recognised this genre as the most popular. Why? Simply because everyone is in search of love, and that is how these films begin: a character, no matter how successful they may seem, if not loved and loving, is leading an empty life.

We need to be careful here in case we assume that love can only be fulfilling as romantic love; this is not so. It is the quality of love which we see in the Trinity, not a particular form of relationship, that is important and life-giving. This essential-ness of love (in whatever relationship) is emphasised by the often fairy-tale quality of 'rom coms'; good fairy tales help us understand what is deep within us. The fresh expressions of church with whom I spoke understand their communities because they really do love people and relate to them. This is, of course, what we would expect; it is a natural outworking of people's experience of God's love.

Finally, let's return to the point made by Hot Chocolate about 'curiosity'. As people get to know their new communities, they discover a curiosity, and not just among youth (though it should be noted that there may be certain generational differences here[15]). There is a real openness and opportunity for us to share our faith in an appropriate way. But there is also a challenge: our words are important in this, and for some of us this is dif-ficult. The 'Talking Jesus' research indicates that this may be more of an issue for those generations older than 'Millennials'.[16]

In talking to people in Scotland, I've sensed that for a num-ber, faith is not only personal, but has also become cripplingly privatised; this privatising has helped foster a false secular/ sacred divide. Whatever the reasons may be – and there are many – this privatising of faith results in our failure to talk about Jesus and share him with others. It stifles naturalness in living out our faith to the full and it blinds us, and others, to Christ being Lord of every part of life.

At the end of Matthew's Gospel account, we have what is often called 'the Great Commission'. It is an incredibly dra-matic moment when the risen, about to ascend Jesus charges his disciples to '. . . go and make disciples . . . '.[17] These words, over the past 2,000 years, have inspired sacrificial mission in the church, and we thank God for those whose obedience to Jesus we would be honoured to follow. However, as we listen to what fresh expressions of church are learning about God, themselves and their community, we hear a helpful reminder of the context in which we live out these words.

We live these words out in the reality that Christ has not only risen, but he has risen and ascended. We sometimes only hear these words in the immediate context in which they were spoken, so we think of going out from where Jesus is. But the ascended Jesus is not limited to one spatial coordinate; he is in all the world in which he calls us to journey.[18] As so many fresh expressions of church recognise, Jesus is already in the community to which they go to serve. In saying, 'Go and make disciples', Jesus is also saying, 'Come follow me',[19] and so he is always with us. The experience of fresh expressions of church bears witness to the assurance that Jesus is lord of all places; his authority is complete, and we can never go to where he is not present.

Notes

1 Orwell, George, *Animal Farm* (London: Secker and Warburg, 1945).

2 Hot Chocolate website www.hotchocolate.org.uk.

3 Hot Chocolate interview.

4 Hot Chocolate interview.

5 Sanctuary First interview.

6 The Shed interview.

7 The Shed interview.

8 St Kentigern's interview.

9 Sparks, Soerens and Friesen, *The New Parish*, p. 56.

10 Hot Chocolate interview.

11 Williams, Rowan, *Faith in the Public Square* (London: Bloomsbury, 2012), p. 17, citing Gaita, R., *Common Humanity: Thinking About Love and Truth and Justice* (Melbourne: Routledge, 1999), p. 24.

12 Gateways interview.

13 St Kentigern's interview.

14 *Mark Kermode's Secrets of Cinema*, first broadcast on BBC 2, 17 July 2018, Episode 1, 'The Rom Com'.

15 See 'Talking Jesus' research, https://talkingjesus.org/research/.

16 We need to be careful that in applying the 'Talking Jesus' findings, we take into account critical regional and national differences. Within the four nations of the UK, there is a different story of engagement between

church and the wider community and, at present, there are significantly different national narratives.

17 Matthew 28:19.

18 Paula Gooder speaks of Jesus inviting us to travel with him and make disciples, Sheffield Diocesan Conference: 'Discipleship in a Christlike Church', 9–11 June 2015. Paula Gooder, 'A Biblical View of Discipleship'; published 12 June 2015, Diocese of Sheffield, YouTube, available online at www.youtube.com/watch?v=EVq4LyxDKgo. Cf. Psalm 139, which speaks of God's universal presence and authority.

19 Matthew 4:19; Mark 1:17; Luke 5:27; John 1:43.

Part 3
Introduction

For those who enjoy the world of superheroes, the Marvel universe is a rich one, be that comic, graphic novel or film. One of the long-standing characters is Professor Charles Xavier, the mentor of the X-Men. One of Xavier's particular gifts is that telepathically he senses the thoughts and emotions of others. In order not to be swamped by this potential cacophony of psychic energy, he must be disciplined and focused. And so it is for us as we survey the world of fresh expressions of church in Scotland and the lessons we are learning – we could easily be swamped by the richness of the experience of others and by their varied voices in expressing this.

So, what we will do in this part is focus on four key areas ('Sharing a Vision', 'Getting Started', 'Discipleship' and 'Parish Life') and listen to a few representative voices as they speak to us from their experience. These voices will in general look beyond the local, as they reflect on what has happened in recent years. Each speaks with their own authentic voice expressing what they are experiencing and observing. Each comes from a particular perspective, which might be markedly different from that of someone else looking at the same topic. This lack of uniformity may be a little challenging for us, but it is an intrinsic consequence of our listening to others and hearing what they are saying, rather than our hearing what we think they should be saying.

What all contributors have in common is experience, mature reflection, passion and something important to share with us. And as they all are listeners, they would not want us to blindly accept what they have written; rather, they would want us to engage constructively with their words, critique what they have said, nuance their observations in the light of our own experience and understanding and then, together as the church of Christ, move forward.

5

Sharing a Vision

With contributions from Tommy MacNeil,
Michael Harvey, Helen Brough, David Logue
and Siân Ashby.

For a generation, *Star Trek* (the original series) was, among other things, the champion of the split infinitive: 'To boldly go', seemed just the way to say it. The phrase was full of adventure, mystery, exploration, friendship and hope. Of course, the adventure could not be contained within one generation, so *Star Trek: The Next Generation* appeared. In the Star Trek universe, there is about a century's gap between the early voyages of Captain Kirk's Starship *Enterprise* and the last of Jean-Luc Picard's Starship *Enterprise*-D. In the world of science fiction, this time difference poses no hurdle for a personal encounter between the two captains. And the story of this encounter is a really helpful one for the exploration of fresh expressions of church.[1]

We begin with a recently retired Captain Kirk, who is somewhat at a loss. He lacks purpose, and disillusionment and even bitterness are ready to take hold. He is invited to the launch of the Starship *Enterprise*-B; the first Enterprise not to be captained by him for over a quarter of a century. During the launch something unexpected happens. The ship is almost destroyed, but Kirk rescues it and is presumed to have been killed as he did so. However, in 'reality', he has been transported to the 'Nexus' zone, a zone in space where time means little and where one's deepest dreams can be realised.

We now flash forward to the world of Captain Picard. He and his crew are desperately trying to save a planet, which is about to be destroyed as the 'villain' of the story attempts to reach the Nexus zone. Only Kirk can help Picard succeed in this rescue. Through the wonders of storytelling he meets Kirk in the, apparent, satisfaction of his world of fantasy. Initially Kirk does not listen; then two things happen. Picard challenges Kirk to remember who he is – he's a starship captain – he calls Kirk to follow him, to make a difference and to save a world that is facing destruction. Second, Kirk realises that the world that he has created around himself is a world of false ease; it is a lie. At one level it is real, but, at core, it is a fantasy that hides, rather than reveals, the depths of reality and what it really means to live.

Kirk leaves with Picard. They save the planet, but in the conflict Kirk is mortally wounded. As he lies dying, he looks up at Picard and asks, 'Did we do it? Did we make a difference?' Picard smiles, 'Yes, we made a difference.'

A local church, like Captain Kirk, can be weary, tired and lose direction and purpose. It can easily create and settle into a world of its own shaping, a world that is comfortable and reassuring – a world without challenge. The adventure of fresh expressions of church reminds us of who and what we are. We hear God call us not to live a lie – a lie, which no matter how appealing, will only lead to emptiness and a waste of life (for us and for others).[2] With the adventure of fresh expressions of church, there is a restoration and sharing of vision, the gift of an opportunity to make a difference and a call to live passionately as we use our gifts and experience. But there is always risk, even the risk of death. Yet, when we close our eyes for the last time and open them for the first, surely we want to look at the face of Jesus and ask Kirk's question, 'Did we do it? Did we make a difference?'; and surely we want to hear the reply, 'Yes, we made a difference.'

Picard and Kirk shared a vision, they trusted one another and they took risks; the same is true in the life of a fresh expression of church. But, how do we share a vision? Let's think about this from two perspectives: first the local and then the regional and national.

Tommy MacNeil writes about the parish experience of Martin's Memorial church in Stornoway.[3]

Releasing a Vision: Martin's Memorial and The Shed Project

Vision. It's an important word. One that can cause all kinds of emotions to stir in our hearts. For some it causes excitement and enthusiasm. For others, it's a sense of dread or even guilt. Some don't like vision as for them it equates change, and people don't like change. Whatever our thoughts regarding vision, the God whom we worship views it as crucial in the life of the church. So much so that he warns us:

> Where there is no vision, the people perish. (Proverbs 29:18; KJV)
> When there is no clear prophetic vision, people quickly wander astray. (TPT)

God clearly views the issue of vision as being of utmost importance in the church. To encourage you to be a person of vision, to encourage us to be a church of vision, I want to share four basic principles that I've learned in recent years. Life and faith lessons that will encourage us to be people who don't just have vision, but who in releasing vision, will see such visions become reality as God brings his life to us.

Principle 1: See Yourself as God Sees You

God is the true visionary. He saw this world and created it with its beauty and complexity. Why make an ocean so deep and a universe so vast that we're still discovering treasures within them? Because God is the ultimate Creator. What

---

he has made reveals, gives vision and clarity as to who he is (Psalm 19:1–2).

This is not just true of creation, it's true of you! God saw you before this world came into being. He had vision of your life before your parents were born. He made you in his image. You reveal something of God to this world that no-one else ever has or ever will. You truly are amazing, a true work of art by God himself (Psalm 139:14). This is why you're a visionary. It's in your DNA. Vision is not just to be found in the creatives, the artists, the dreamers. Vision is for all people.

When you begin to see yourself as God sees you, and when you have an awareness of what he's put inside of you, that's when vision, dreams, purpose, destiny, future become part of who you are. It's who you were created to be. Vision releases life. Part of God's vision for your life is that he uses you to allow others to have vision for the change you want to see around you. You need to be the change you want to see! God longs to give you vision for your life, your church and your community.

Principle 2: Seeing What God Sees

What do you see when you look at your church? What about your community? When we speak about releasing a vision, often our first response is to think within the walls and structure of our own congregation. There is one major problem with that; it is far too restrictive, which in turn leads to having too small a vision. God isn't interested in just tweaking or changing your church, he has vision for transforming your community! We need to come in line with God's vision for us.

As we looked within our church, we saw much to encourage us and to be thankful for; a growing congregation, welcoming new people regularly, thriving children's and youth work – the list went on and on. However, when we looked at our community and asked God to show us what he saw, it was at best challenging, and at worst it was devastating. Family breakdown, poverty, addiction, mental health issues, self-harm, long-term unemployment, and again, the list could go on and on.

What could we do? We reminded ourselves that God doesn't just so love the church, he so loved the world! With that truth in our hearts, we began to ask God for ways in which we could best love and serve our community. We began to see purpose, hope, potential, etc. Our vision was changing. We weren't just seeing the problems; we were seeing people and the possibility of new beginnings for them. As we saw this vision of new life, we began to see a new space, a neutral space, a non-church, non-religious space that could become church as it was shaped not by us, but by the people who needed it. We began to see The Shed. God shared his heart with us, not just for a new building, but for new communities of hope, and we were ready to run with it.

There are two main types of vision. That which we see with our eyes, and that which we see with our hearts. In the life of the church, the latter part of vision is every bit as important as the former.

In 2 Kings 6 we have the rather amusing account of Elisha's servant waking up and opening his eyes to see the hills around them filled with enemy forces (2 Kings 6:15). That's it; they were done for, he thought. Interestingly, Elisha prays for his servant, 'O Lord, open his eyes so that he may see.' How does this make sense? Elisha's servant was gripped with fear because of what his eyes initially saw.

We know of course that Elisha's prayer was to do with the eyes of the heart. He needed to see what God saw. God opened his spiritual eyes, and he saw the hills full of horses and chariots, the Lord's army. Seeing what God saw took away fear and replaced it with renewed faith and hope for the future. We need to see as God sees.

Colonel Thomas Edward Lawrence (Lawrence of Arabia) was a soldier in World War One. He said,

All men dream but not equally. Those who dream by night in the dusty recesses of their minds awake to the day to find it was all vanity. But the dreamers of the day are dangerous men and women, for they may act out their dreams with open eyes, to make it possible . . .[4]

What does God want you to see? Ask him to open the eyes of your heart.

Principle 3: Say What You See

This is often the most challenging aspect of releasing a vision. All true vision begins in God's heart. He then makes his heart vulnerable by sharing it with us and giving us the option as to whether we receive it and run with it or not (Habakkuk 2:2–3).

All God-given vision requires faith to see it become reality. As well as faith, such vision requires words. The Bible tells us that the power of life and death are in the tongue (Proverbs 18:21). For vision to come alive, the vision needs to be spoken.

When God created the world, he didn't think it into being, he spoke it into being ('And God said!' – Genesis 1:3, 6, 9, 11, 14, 20, 24 . . .). We need to follow his example.

In the first few years of my ministry in Martin's Memorial, most of our growth was among young people. This was encouraging and challenging. We recognised that God was doing something significant among our youth, and we had a sense of responsibility in shaping and investing into the future of this work. We had reached a limit in terms of existing space in our church, so we were looking outside for options. There was an old derelict building to the rear of our church.

God began to give me vision for how we could use this space. I remember hearing a sermon a few years ago that stated, 'nothing happens in God's kingdom and in the world without a declaration'. In view of this truth, and in light of God's example in creation, I took our youth worker to the rear wall of our church and pointed to the derelict building. I asked him, 'How would you like that to become a dedicated youth and community building so that we can develop our youth church?' He was excited at the prospect, but looking at the old derelict building my words appeared at best to be unrealistic, and at worst that I wasn't hearing right from God.

This was one of our most crucial moments in turning vision into reality. I had to step out in faith and use words to give life to what I was seeing in my heart.

The next stage was sharing the vision with our church leadership. I did this knowing that we were paying off a £135,000 loan to the General Trustees and that this new building would likely cost something in the region of £250,000–300,000. At that point, we had no land, no money, no reserves, but we had vision. As we gave words to the vision, the miracle that is The Shed Project began to unfold. New life had begun. We now have three youth workers and an army of volunteers involved in the youthwork aspect of The Shed. The work continues to grow and develop.

Put words to what you see in your heart and watch with wonder as it takes life.

Principle 4: Sow into What You See
Having spoken about what God has shown you, the next crucial stage in seeing vision become reality is to start sowing

into the vision. Faith and words are just the beginning of releasing a vision. There are other crucial elements involved.

Prayer is an essential ingredient. Another crucial element is a correct sense of timing. When we receive fresh vision, we're often in a hurry to see it realised. God is never in a hurry, and his timing is always perfect. Then there's the need for wisdom for the practicalities of the vision unfolding, and not forgetting the financing of the vision.

The great missionary Hudson Taylor was a man of profound vision. One of his main life lessons was 'God's work done in God's way will never lack God's supply'. This quote was in a journal he wrote while reflecting about God's work in China.

> Our heavenly Father is a very experienced One. He knows very well that His children wake up with a good appetite every morning . . . He sustained 3 million Israelites in the wilderness for 40 years. We do not expect He will send 3 million missionaries to China; but if He did, He would have ample means to sustain them all![5]

In the church I would rather have vision without money, than money without vision. We've discovered that to have no option but to rely on God for the fulfilment of a vision is actually a gift. We watch a miracle unfold before us, and we continue to look to God and trust him for the growth of what he's called into being.

Be prepared to sow into your vision. Sow your prayers, your preaching, your heart, your faith, your time and your energy into the vision. When you do that, you'll then be able to call others to join with you in sowing finances into it. We are not an overly wealthy congregation, yet in a six-year period (2009–14) we spent £600,000 turning vision into reality. Last year (2017) we as a leadership had vision for paying off all outstanding debt. This we did, and we have now released fresh vision for our next major capital project: the refurbishing of our church hall along with installing a new purpose-built kitchen. This will enable us to develop our work further, especially in building better links with our community. We estimate the cost of this to be £350,000 (approx.). We don't have the money, but our recent history has taught us that as long as we have vision, and that such vision originated with God, he will do what he did at the beginning of our world. He speaks and new life begins.

What vision would God have you release for your church and community? I assure you that in God our greatest days are always ahead of us. He's excited by your future, and so should you be. Why don't you ask him about it?

Be prepared that when he speaks, you need to be ready to speak. As you do, as you release vision, God will help you create a new future. Not just for you, but for your church, your community and for the people around you whom he loves so much.

Tommy MacNeil

When Tommy writes, 'Vision is for all people', he's expressing a confidence that, because of who God is, how we are created and the nature we have been given, we all have the potential to share in God's mission. Partnership and co-ownership should be expected. From the experience of Martin's Memorial and The Shed, sharing a vision with others means having confidence:

- That God has a vision for a particular community.
- In how we are created: in God's image, as intrinsic bearers of vision.
- That God will share with us, at least in part, the Creator's heart for and understanding of a community.

- That God calls us to share in the divine vision for a particular community.
- To act upon what God has shown to us and take the risks involved in this.
- To love, listen and serve the community, with the community: as a part of it.
- To communicate openly and well with everyone involved, thereby minimising misunderstanding.
- To be humble with others and with God. Pray continually, not just at the beginning of a venture. There is a temptation once a process has got under way to rest upon our experience or gifts. The experience of The Shed is to continually pray and bring the detail to God; everything is in total dependence upon him.
- To trust God through 'thick and thin'.

As Tommy speaks of their experience in Stornoway, there is openness, excitement and a sense of expectancy in his voice and heart. This contrasts with a guardedness that, all too often, accompanies mission; but, why this guardedness? The answer is many-threaded, but let's pick out three parts of the weave: defensiveness, a misunderstanding of purity, and risk.

In all three, an awareness of the role of fear is very important, so we'll look at this first, then we'll briefly think about defensiveness and purity. Risk we'll consider in more depth in Part 4.

Michael Harvey, the Chief Executive of the National Weekend of Invitation, has wide experience in helping Christians face their fears regarding mission. Reflecting on faith, imagination and fear, he writes:[6]

Bringing Faith to Our Imagination and Facing Our Fear

Joe, I want you to ask God, 'Is there someone you want me to have a God conversation with?' This is the question

---

I have been asking individual Christians in Scotland and England over the past six months. The results have been revealing. Seventy per cent of those Christians immediately see the person in their mind's eye, and almost instantaneously their first response is a fearful one. Words and phrases such as apprehensive, challenging, trepidation, an intense reticence, tension, reluctance, scary and nervous come to mind. These phrases or words are then followed by the reason for their fear. One minister said their fear was of the person not liking the act of worship. A fear of not being good enough, a fear of a hostile reaction or fear of being asked a difficult question . . . Fear of inadequacy. I noticed how quickly the person would exit the present moment and revisit an experience of their past, and imagine the future based on the past.

Whether we are a Christian in a fresh expression of church or attending a Sunday act of worship, we are not immune to the call of God suddenly bursting forth, compelling us to have a God conversation with someone. What happens next so often is a mixture of imagination and fear, and that is where the call of God so often ends. Søren Kierkegaard taught that humanity advances on the backs of those rare geniuses who venture into realms of which most of us are afraid. Answering the call of God to go and have a God conversation is where most fresh expressions start, but I wonder whether we have taught one another that the first initial call to set up a fresh expression of church will be followed by mini calls to advance into realms of which we are afraid?

There is an aspect of fear that contains a God-given imagination and there is an aspect of fear that misuses imagination and elevates us into the position of God. Theologian A. W. Tozer wrote an article back in 1959 on the value of a sanctified imagination.

The sacred gift of seeing, the ability to peer beyond the veil and gaze with astonished wonder upon the beauties and mysteries of things holy and eternal.[7]

And Tozer points in the Bible to the Gospel of John,

But when he, the Spirit of truth, comes, he will guide you into all the truth. He will not speak on his own; he will speak only what he hears, and he will tell you what is yet to come. He will glorify me because it is from me that he will receive what he will make known to you. (John 16:13–14; NIV)

There are two different Hebrew words used for fear in the Old Testament: *'pachad'*, which means panic, and *'yirah'*, which is used more than any other word for fear (forty-four times). *Yirah*, which is translated 'don't be afraid', is a very different concept than panic; it is recognising a holy fear that is difficult to translate but has three aspects:

1. Inhabiting a larger space that is bigger than usual, a space that is exhilarating and terrifying at the same time.
2. We have a surge of energy.
3. We are aware of the presence of God.

This can be seen clearly with Moses at the burning bush where despite panicking about the request from God in the end, after a lengthy conversation, he obeys after God says, 'I will go down with you to Egypt but bring you back up' (Genesis 46:4; NASB).

God offers this to every human being that, despite our fear, he goes with us on the journey.

So there is a fear that keeps us alive and fear that keeps us from living. *Pachad* is the fear that keeps us from living.

This fear tethers us to an unlived life, and one might spell the *Pachad* type of fear as:

FUTURE
EVENT
ALREADY
RUINED

Any strategy that keeps us from facing our fear is a mistake in the long run. If you avoid a fear for too long, it will own you.

Yirah, however, is the holy fear that challenges us to live. So often I have seen in my own life and also in the lives of others that the path to one's greatest potential is straight through our greatest fear. Most of the transformation moments in our lives have been accompanied by the feeling of fear of the activity as we have imagined it going horribly wrong. God wanted the best for the children of Israel when the twelve spies entered Canaan (Numbers chapters 13—14). However, only two of the twelve faced their fears and were able to see the future as God was planning it. The best is often on the other side of fear! For as it says in Proverbs 9:10, 'For the fear of the LORD is the beginning of wisdom' (NIV).

So how do we reframe our relationship with that which we don't control? For if we don't reframe our fear of something or someone, it can paralyse. Our model, I would suggest, must be Jesus. Jesus said, 'Very truly I tell you, the Son can do nothing by himself; he can do only what he sees his Father doing, because whatever the Father does the Son also does' (John 5:19; NIV).

In practical terms, this is the contemplative practice of accessing God's direction as a strategy for mission and the extension of the kingdom of God.

I think Jesus in the garden of Gethsemane is our behavioural model for bringing faith to our imagination when we face a destructive fear.

- Social support: Jesus enhanced his social support by taking his friends with him.
- Express emotion: he began to be troubled and sorrowful.
- Cope actively: he prayed to his Father.
- Alter your perception: 'Take this cup from me. Yet not what I will, but what you will.'
- Face rather than flee the fear: 'Rise! Let us go! Here comes my betrayer!'

Jesus knows or imagines what is coming as he withdraws in the Garden of Gethsemane and He asks for the task to be taken away, but if not then may God's will be done. Jesus deals with a fear of the future, imagining the outcome with obedience and faces his fear. At times, we will have to reimagine the future or reframe it as we become more aware of God's plan. Either way, like Jesus,

FACE
ALTER
COPE
EXPRESS
SOCIAL SUPPORT

Joe, I want you to ask God, 'Is there someone you want me to have a God conversation with?'

You hear the call to go to someone.
You instantaneously feel the fear that this could go wrong.

But you remember through your imagination that God is
with you and has just called you.
You pray to God to make sure you have heard right.
You ask for strength.
You use faith to face fear and answer the call of God.

Michael Harvey

As we return to briefly think about how defensiveness and a
misunderstanding of purity can negatively affect our engagement with mission, a question: is the glass half-full, half-empty
or both?[8] It would be easy to caricature fresh expressions of
church as made up of people whose glass is half-full, but this,
in my experience, is not always the case. What does seem to
be the case is that they share an appreciation of what is in the
glass and, without being naïve, they focus on positive possibilities. Their listening to a community means that, as well as
seeing its strength and life, they cannot do other than face up
to the vulnerability, pain and wrong in that community.

So NYNO (Neither Young Nor Old) is a fresh expression of
church where illness and death are easily evident; Hot Chocolate
is a community where isolation and loneliness are a common
experience. These groups are not naïve. They are, however,
groups that are not cowed by these experiences; rather than
being fretfully self-protective, they are centres of hope. They
are not taken aback or put on the defensive by the realities of
human nature; they understand the reality of evil, but they look
for the best, and from this perspective they challenge that which
is destructive. They seek, first, the image of God in people,
rather than the fracture of sin. This approach allows them to be
open and to be released from fear; free to embrace and not be
defensive.

Neil Cole reminds us that the gates of a fortress or a city are
defensive, rather than offensive, structures.[9] In the light of this,
when Jesus speaks of the gates of hell not prevailing against

the church,[10] while it may not justify images of the church militant on the attack, it does underscore the authority of Jesus; it points to the impotence of death when faced with the power of the resurrection. Jesus' words call us to a confidence in the life that he has given us and to a profound peace in the sharing of this. This assurance, rather than fear, characterises the intuition and the stories of many of the fresh expressions of church that I meet. Their instinct and default is for the open road of adventure, not the silo of a besieged fortress.

Purity is important, but what does this mean in the reality of life in our complex world? Being a disciple, as we shall see later, is about being transformed to be more like Jesus. It is a path of holiness and increasing purity, which allows the image of God to blaze within us. But this purity is not solely expressed in the domain of the individual, it is also at the heart of the church.

A fear of compromising this purity, this image of God, is understandable, but what type of fear is it? As Michael Harvey asked us earlier, is the fear we face 'Pachad' or 'Yirah', a fear that destroys or a fear that frees us to live? If it is the former, it will spread the corrosive acid of anxious reserve and fear of 'contamination'; it will scar us and others as we engage in mission. The root of this life-denying fear could be due to a variety of reasons, for example, because of a church culture which, over time, has been shaped by a pastoring and discipling that has misunderstood the Biblical perspectives on holiness, mission and the relationship between the two,[11] or it could be from a lack of confidence in God, or from pride and a seeking of reputation and status.

Another potential area of tension regarding 'purity' is when the ideals of fresh expressions of church seem to be threatened by the realities of the context. Vincent Donovan was a Roman Catholic priest who spent fifteen years (1958–73) as a missionary among the Maasai in northern Tanzania; he wrote about his experiences in *Christianity Rediscovered*.[12] The book describes his heart to enculturate the gospel into a local context. In 2006, John Bowen journeyed to Tanzania to see what had happened after Donovan had left:

Vincent Donovan was a visionary, and *Christianity Rediscovered* describes not only what actually happened but
what he believed should have happened . . . Since he left, his
friends and colleagues have taken his ideals and, over several
decades of faithful service, have worked at grounding his
ideals in the realities of life in Maasailand. It is impossible to
say how he would have adapted to the problems they have
encountered – the difficulties of ordaining Maasai leaders,
the need for ongoing pastoral care, an unsympathetic church
hierarchy, the encroaching destruction of the Maasai way of
life, and the need for education and medical care. Maybe he
could not have made the transition from pioneering to maintenance, from vision to reality: it seems not to have been his
gift . . . [Others], however, were not the visionaries but the
implementers of the vision. In the body of Christ, both are
necessary.[13]

Bowen's observations raise a number of important points, but
our focus is on the tension between vision and reality, a tension
that has the potential to snap the cord of fellowship and the
capacity to stunt the growth of a nascent expression of church.
This axis of tension can arise both between inherited and fresh
expressions of church and, perhaps more surprisingly, from
within a new expression of church, for example, when some
from within the new context want a model of church, which
goes back to their memory and expectations of church and
does not fully reflect the culture of the community, as the pioneers perceive it to be.

What does proper compromise look like? We'll pick this up
later when we think about discipleship and consider what a
'principled' or 'virtuous' pragmatism might mean. Suffice to
say that, in sharing a vision with others, we must embrace reality: the good and the bad, the clear and the confusing, the light
and the dark and all that weaves between. We are not thinking about theoretical possibilities, but about what can actually
happen, what can be lived out in practice, at this moment in

this context. In vision, mission and hope we always say, like Morpheus in the film *The Matrix*, 'Welcome to the real world'.

The aphorism 'Culture eats strategy for breakfast'[14] has perhaps become a bit of a cliché, but it expressed a crucial insight for us in the Church of Scotland when, five years ago, we began to think how we could, in practice, encourage and support the development of fresh expressions of church. There were many good suggestions, enthusiastically put forward, but we were at risk of 'dying the death of a hundred good ideas'. We didn't have the resources to do all that was suggested. However, even more chastening was that we could be incredibly busy, but, in reality, achieve very little that would bear fruit. When new resources are dedicated to an initiative, there is always the temptation to feel the need to 'prove ourselves'. We resisted this and focused on the question of how we could help our church develop a culture that would encourage the growth of fresh expressions of church.

As mentioned earlier, our motivation is key; but so is our perception of the story in which we find ourselves. By this I mean, not just the big story of God's grace, but also the specific episode in which we find ourselves at this precise moment.

In the film of the book *One Flew over the Cuckoo's Nest*,[15] there is a scene where the 'hero' of the film, McMurphy, helps a group of patients escape from a brutally-run ward in a psychiatric hospital. They go down to the harbour, board a boat and are standing on deck ready to set sail when they are challenged. Confusion and panic begin to cross their faces, and then McMurphy takes charge of the situation. He introduces them, one by one, as doctors. Two things happen. First, a look of confidence and ease replaces that of fear, as his companions see themselves in a new light. Second, those who are questioning them now treat them with a new-found respect. It is a very telling moment in the movie; the story being told affects perception.

It is the same for us in the church: the story we believe affects how we perceive ourselves and, in turn, how we act. What narrative are we a part of: inevitable decline, or adventure, celebration and growth? Are we guardians of ever-limited resources, or heralds of the kingdom; managers of nostalgia, or explorers of a new world? If our culture is not one of openness and expectancy, then strategies for sharing vision will fail. In all of this, there must be honesty: the story must be told 'warts and all', but what is the story?

When we met, five years ago, we believed that, although there were significant problems and areas of failure and vulnerability within the church, our story was not one of retreat. So, the challenge was how to communicate this and effect culture change based on this perception. To help us strategically do this we developed a process, which we called 'Going for Growth'. But, before looking at this in more detail, let's take a little detour and pick up on a word that Bowen used of Vincent Donovan and his work in Tanzania: 'pioneering'. What does it mean, to have pioneering at the heart of our story?

The word pioneer can have many cultural connotations, some of which may not sit easily with how it's generally understood in the world of fresh expressions of church in the UK. Further, like the word 'fresh' it can be heard by some as implying a deficiency in them; unfortunately, at times, this has been unfairly implied by the one speaking. Yet, if we are honest, there are times when we do need to recognise that we have become settled in an unhealthy way. There are times when we have avoided challenge and change not just for our immediate ease, but because of something deeper: we have let our sense of identity become intimately entwined with the status quo.[16] Our experience in Scotland is a mixture: some inherited expressions of church that have initiated a fresh expression have a strong tradition of innovative mission; others have needed gentle encouragement; and some have needed the spark of renewal to catch this vision. What is important is to be honest, open to the Spirit of God and then to be obedient.

From her parish experience and her work with Forge Scotland, Helen Brough speaks of the importance of pioneering, how it is a key gift to the church, yet only functions effectively in interdependence with other gifts and callings.[17] She helps us understand some of the challenges that come, particularly if we are just beginning to glimpse the excitement of pioneering and tentatively take our first step.

Pioneer Leadership: More Than a Job Title

Pioneer . . . an innovator, ground breaker, trailblazer, pathfinder, front runner, founder, architect, experimenter, instigator, explorer, discoverer.[18]

How do you hear or respond to those descriptors? What do they provoke in you? Excitement, resonance, hope, vision, affirmation or something more complex, mixed with fatigue, caution, fear and a sense of 'yes . . . but . . .'?

And let us run with perseverance the race marked out for us, fixing our eyes on Jesus, the pioneer and perfecter of faith . . . (Hebrews 12:1–2; NIV)

The body of Christ has been created to move, but my sense is that though there is the heart to move in light of the missional context we find ourselves in, the reality of actually moving is different. Far from the picture in Hebrews 12 of us straining towards the line as seasoned athletes, we find we have a dead leg having sat comfortably for too long! Getting up from sitting, we discover that the legs we assumed we could put weight on, aren't 'there'. We realise that the only route to weight bearing is to begin to move and to go through the uncomfortable pins and needles sensation until some sense of normality is restored. Even after that, we limp for a while until power and sensation are restored!

This, I believe, is the state we find ourselves in as the church in Scotland. Having got up to stand, we find our ability to bear weight and move is compromised. What is apparent though is the pain and discomfort of the pins and needles, and the frustration of not being able to move as hoped. The reality of getting moving is uncomfortable – the pain is real. The whole body feels it. Enabling the body of Christ to fully move again will be a costly task, as the writer to the Hebrews recognised, but one that will bring restoration, life and movement beyond what we have recently known. It's time to 'strengthen your feeble arms and weak knees. "Make level paths for your feet, so that the lame may not be disabled, but rather healed"' (Hebrews 12:12–13; NIV).

My conviction is that we need to enable the whole body of Christ to be mobilised – and this won't happen without being far more intentional about identifying, giving permission to, training, equipping, supporting, advocating for and learning from the innovators. We need to positively engage with the legs that have been 'sat on'. Current trends indicate that our failure to move as God intended has meant the church has drifted away from wider society.

The recent Barna research[19] assessing the state of Christianity, faith and church in Scotland, highlighted that:

- 49 per cent identified as those of another/no faith
- 51 per cent self-identified as Christian – of which
  - 69 per cent legacy Christians
  - 26 per cent non-evangelical born again Christians
  - 5 per cent self-identified as evangelical Christians (as defined according to the Bebbington rubric).

So what does this mean in practice? What will it take to get moving?

To break the inertia we find ourselves in, and begin to tackle the missional opportunity that there is before us, will require us to change our focus as to who we equip to lead and how we do this.

The terms 'leader' and 'leadership' are often used interchangeably, Dalakoura helpfully articulates and contrasts the individual nature of leader development with leadership, which she articulates, 'is a complex phenomenon that encompasses the interactions between the leader and the social and organisational environment'.[20]

The vast majority of our training programmes for church leadership see leaders as individuals, train them in isolation from their contexts and have failed to enable them to work effectively in teams.

Further, for change to come, it's imperative that we broaden our thinking of who should lead. The skills and expertise required to break new ground are vastly different from those required to maintain the status quo.

There is one body and one Spirit, just as you were called to one hope when you were called; one Lord, one faith, one baptism; one God and Father of all, who is over all and through all and in all. But to each one of us grace has been given as Christ apportioned it . . . So Christ himself gave the apostles, the prophets, the evangelists, the pastors and teachers, to equip his people for works of service, so that the body of Christ may be built up until we all reach unity in the faith and in the knowledge of the Son of God and become mature, attaining to the whole measure of the fullness of Christ. (Ephesians 4:4–7, 11–13; NIV)

In his unpacking of Ephesians 4, the missional thinker Alan Hirsch[21] articulates the synergy of the apostolic, prophetic, evangelistic, shepherding and teaching roles. They are all vital for the growing, maturing and multiplying of the body of Christ – and yet, we have largely valued and trained the shepherds and teachers to lead in the church. We have largely ignored the more pioneering roles of the apostle, prophet and evangelist – many of whom have found greater freedom to break new ground in parachurch or mission organisations.

The context we're in demands a level of innovation and entrepreneurial skills that go beyond what we currently have in place. But these are callings in themselves. Superimposing them on those of another 'wiring' through a job description is not sufficient to get the job done. We need to identify, give permission to, train, connect and resource those of a more apostolic, prophetic, evangelistic wiring who will pioneer.

Below are three elements that I believe are key in restoring movement to the body of Christ as God designed it:

Identifying the Pioneers

In one sense this is easy: they are the ones who can't but help start things, be it in the home, work place or community. They question the status quo, thrive on new ideas, vision, possibilities and change. The complicating factor is that they will often self-censor within the church environment, which values stability. They can also be those who create friction as they question what currently is. This is uncomfortable – and the greatest temptation is to shut this down, but it's vitally important – it's the pins and needles chapter of getting functional again! Taking the time and courage to listen to their questions, thoughts and ideas is key in beginning to restore movement.

For all of us who follow Christ, regardless of the sphere of influence we have, character is key, but it is particularly so for those of us who lead. Regardless of which of the fivefold roles we lean to (or whatever personality profiling tools we use), we cannot escape the fact that there are strengths and vulnerabilities to all of these capabilities. As humans we all have strengths, fragilities and limits. Often these are not things we willingly embrace, particularly as leaders, but it is imperative for the health of the body of Christ that we do.

Starting new things is tough. Character, authenticity, integrity, resilience and the willingness/ability to learn and relearn are all vital to staying the course.

Permission, Advocating and Resourcing

We speak of what we value, and our language shapes culture. When we have identified pioneers, it's essential we explicitly give them permission to pioneer and affirm, encourage them in this. They will bring change, require resourcing, and not everything they begin will take off. These things are a great challenge to a risk-averse culture which values stability. Very practically, for people to pioneer, they need to be released from tasks they may have been attending to, so that they have the space to initiate the new thing.

Training and Connecting

Through the years of training pioneers in Forge, it's become clear that the in-context training of pioneering teams by practitioner-teachers is the most effective means of seeing new missional projects and ecclesial communities birthed. Pioneers are experiential learners and when given the opportunity to be trained with other pioneers, they flourish and develop relational networks that will bear fruit as they pioneer. It is also vital that there is ongoing connection with and coaching by those more experienced. Having access to communities of like-minded people to sustain, learn together and share 'just in time learning' is vital when you're breaking new ground.

A Few Words of Warning

A note to the planners in life – change is not linear – it's complex. We cannot control innovation. Pioneers bring change. This will not be a surprise, but often as things begin to change, we suddenly realise how deeply held our values are. It is vital that we hold on to the big picture to get through the pain. As risk is embraced, it is costly, but the sense of kingdom possibilities that is restored to the body with movement is of infinite value.

Pioneer leadership is more than a job title – it is vital to helping local Christian communities find their legs once more.

If we recover our pioneering apostolic, prophetic and evangelist voices, and bring them together with the shepherd and teacher ones, then the body of Christ has the potential to become mature and maybe our communities will say of Christ's church: 'How beautiful on the mountains are the feet of the messenger who brings good news, the good news of peace and salvation, the news that the God of Israel reigns!' (Isaiah 52:7; NLT)

Helen Brough

When, within the Church of Scotland, we developed the national initiative 'Going for Growth' it was important that the process that evolved was coherent with the ethos and manner of fresh expressions of church. In all that we did, and continue to do, from local to international, we have endeavoured to retain this integrity. This has meant

- Ensuring that we go to where people are
- Listening to all who would engage with us
- Hospitality
- Being challenged and challenging
- Advocacy, not merely the communication of a concept
- Encouraging

- Developing relationships, which would deepen understanding and promote action
- Developing, where wanted, ongoing partnerships.

In practice, this meant that 'Going for Growth' developed as a three-year process, which incorporated three core elements.

First, over a three-year period we offered to visit every presbytery in Scotland (at times this would be in small presbytery groupings of three or four). During these visits, we would do two things. In the afternoon, we would meet with those who had presbytery responsibilities. This was important for a number of reasons:

- We wanted to honour the role that these folk had and share with them before we shared with local churches in their areas.
- We wanted to learn from them more about the local contexts before we met with members of local churches.
- We wanted to hear their hopes and concerns.
- We wanted to challenge and encourage them not just to be 'permission givers' (that was too passive and did not appropriately honour their role), but to be those who 'prepared the ground and stood with' those who were developing fresh expressions of church in a local context.
- We wanted to encourage them and help them access all the resources and help that was available.

The afternoon was followed by an evening gathering to which we invited two members from each of the churches within the respective presbyteries to meet with us. At this meeting, we listened, advocated a vision, challenged, encouraged and offered follow-up. Between the afternoon and evening meetings we had also invited everyone who wanted, to have a meal with us. This hospitality was important, not only because some folk had to travel quite a distance, but also because it allowed us more time and context to build relationships.

The second core element reflected our enthusiasm to build ongoing relationships with parishes and presbyteries; we did not want to merely 'parachute' into an area and then disappear. So, we offered the churches in each presbytery, or group of presbyteries, the opportunity of a follow-up Vision Day focused on fresh expressions of church. The first day of meetings was generally in the autumn, and the Vision Days were in the spring. This allowed time, between the days, for us to meet with individual churches, who may have wanted to work things through at a local level. It also allowed time for presbyteries to communicate with local churches that had not chosen, or not been able to meet with us in the autumn.[22]

The autumn presbytery and local church day was run by partnerships from within the Church of Scotland, but the spring Vision Event day was developed with other Fresh Expression partners in Scotland and, as such, was open to all churches, whatever the denomination. The Vision Day was a much more comprehensive look at fresh expressions of church; the day in the autumn was, by virtue of engaging with two different groupings, more limited in time. Also, it had included looking at other resources and forms of mission within the Church of Scotland.

The third element to 'Going for Growth' was a series of three summer schools – national events open to all, with a very specific purpose and ethos. Over three years, we covered the core theology and practice of fresh expressions of church. Each year's content, while being stand-alone, also built upon that of the previous year. We wanted the summer schools to be times of honesty and community; to encourage this we held each over four days and capped the number of participants to fifty-five. We ensured input was of the highest quality and that the dynamic was the optimum mix of plenary, group and one-to-one. These events were both significantly fruitful and, as well, were incredibly enjoyable. They modelled the heart of fresh expressions of church, and they gathered momentum year by year.

Experience of Summer School

Let's listen to two folk who were at all three of the summer schools; first David Logue of the 'Boomer' generation and then Siân Ashby a 'Millennial'.

David writes,[23]

'You've done what?' said my wife with a certain degree of surprise and confusion. 'I have booked us in to that course thing I mentioned – a Church of Scotland summer school about "Going for Growth"', I replied with confidence arising from an assurance that this would be a worthwhile experience for both of us. We are members of a very small church in a rural setting on the west coast of Argyll.

We had retired from proper work about nine months earlier and had been pottering and praying and thinking about what to do with our lives now that the constraints of paid employment, the long hours and brain space that this took up, were behind us. Surely, we could do something in the exercise of our faith and the call of Christ with the rest of our lives which lay before us.

'Going for Growth', exploring new ways of being church, sharing our faith in our community, these flickers of light in the summer school flier appealed to us as potential waymarks for our life ahead.

Three summer schools later, by June 2017, we were sure that this was absolutely the right decision – to go, to go again and to complete the full set.

The first year – setting out the vision and reality of what is happening across Britain – and further – in the growth of new ways of being church, of the birth of communities of Christian faith, brought home to me the possibilities of reaching out beyond the 'church is what happens on Sunday mornings' mindset to go to where people are, to communicate

---

in meaningful context, what the life of a calling to follow Jesus is all about and the freedom and joy which this brings.

Returning home after the first week, we had an encouraging report-back meeting with our church session, which started others thinking and praying also about how to turn round our ageing and declining attendance and to engage with, and serve, our surrounding population.

This week started us on a further journey to find out more, to look creatively at our own parish situation, our context, and to re-evaluate our current fresh expression of Messy Church, and also helped inspire our session's decision to establish a weekly cafe – Cafe Connect – to reconnect with a part of our parish that had no live connection with our church.

Messy Church now regularly has attendance in excess of our Sunday services and is mainly a group of adults and children who would never have dreamt of going to a 'church service'. Our Cafe Connect has now been running weekly for over two years and is eagerly anticipated with over twenty people – some younger, some elderly, some isolated – regularly catching up with one another and re-establishing a community.

The purpose is the church serving the community, no more, no less. That is our answer to those who ask 'Why are you doing this?' After eighteen months, we laid out some Alpha leaflets and let people ask what they were about. From this, we have held three Alpha courses and these have led to 'Alpha Next', a house group of people who completed the Alpha and want to keep meeting. As was often said at the summer school, many people are seeking spirituality, but wouldn't think of looking for this in the local church. We need to go to them in their places and social groups.

But these summer schools were not conferences of individuals looking for information. Almost immediately on arrival, the atmosphere was of sharing, of expectation, of joy at being together in a place where we would grow together. Serious and continuing friendships were founded and invaluable connections made. The talk was of church as community, and this was worked out among us in practice. The end of the first week set the pattern: on the final afternoon, after the communion service, people were reluctant to leave and little groups formed to discuss ideas and experiences, and more specifically, to pray for one another before we parted.

For the second summer school, we were joined enthusiastically by our minister, and attending the third week was never in doubt.

Jesus' command to us is to 'make disciples', leave it to him to build his church. The message from the final summer school is that, fine as activities are, unless we disciple people into 'followers of Jesus' in their communities, unless we grow people into faith in Christ, then we fall short of our calling. That is our challenge with our Messy Church and our Alpha Next.

These summer schools have set us on a journey, they encouraged us on the way and they set our direction for years to come. We look forward with excitement as to what God is going to do next in our wee parish.

David Logue

Siân reflects on her experience:[24]

And those who danced were thought insane by those who could not hear the music. (Anon.)

I first came across this phrase when I was taking salsa classes – it was posted on the class website – and I loved it. It reminds me of the beauty and wildness of God, who calls us to dance with him and to his music, irrespective of what those around us might think. Fresh Expressions of church can be a bit like that. It's risky and messy. It's not contained in nice, neat boxes and, let's face it, it may at times seem a little mad. And I love it.

For a long time, I've felt drawn to the wild edges, the unsettled places of faith. I feel passionately about people knowing the God who loves them: however, I find it frustrating that at times we insist that people adopt what is simply church culture rather than relate to God himself. What would church look like if it sprang from our local context and culture, rather than the other way around?

I wanted to learn more and explore this concept of Fresh Expressions more deeply, so I signed up for the first summer school. I wasn't disappointed – in fact, I enjoyed it so much that I signed up for the next two! What follows are a few reflections on my time spent at the three summer schools, 2015–17.

There are lots of good things I could say about the summer schools – the calibre of the speakers was high, the content stimulating and there was a good balance of theology and real-life experience. However, let me focus on a few key things, which a couple of years down the line still stand out for me.

I really enjoyed the sense of community that built up, both during the course of each summer school and progressively over the three years (a significant proportion of folks attended all three summers). It was wonderful to be able to catch up with people a year down the road and say: 'Well, how did it go?' 'How did that idea we discussed a year ago pan out?'

There was also a sense that each year built on the one previous to it. We began with some of the basics, including the theological foundations for fresh expression of Church, moved on to listening and understanding our context and then concluded with looking at discipleship in fresh expression contexts. This was extremely helpful, as each year added to, and developed, previous knowledge, giving a well-rounded picture by the end of year three.

I appreciated the spaces set aside for personal reflection. I particularly remember one summer, looking at various pictures of Christ taken from different cultures, societies and eras. Most of the pictures were new to me and some were challenging – even shocking. Who is this Christ who spans cultures, time and space? I reflected anew on the question posed to Peter: 'Who do you say I am?' (Matthew 16:15; NIV)

However, probably the most exciting thing for me was to see the changes that occurred in our thinking and mindsets over the three years. At the beginning of the first conference, much of the discussion and questions centred around perceived obstacles: 'What about ordination?' 'What about communion?' We grappled with these. As the week progressed, we focused much more on opportunities – we began to dream: 'What if . . .?' There was a sense of excitement and anticipation, a sense of something new being birthed within the Church of Scotland.

This grew and developed over the three years, and by the end of year three I felt there was also a greater sense of confidence. It wasn't that we suddenly all thought that we could do it on our own; I think we all knew that it would require a deep dependency on God, but there was a right sense of confidence and belief that actually this was possible and achievable – not just 'pie in the sky' stuff. And that maybe we could actually do it.

So what difference has all this made? Where am I now with the whole concept of Fresh Expressions, and what am I doing differently? This past year has been one of great change (I'm now living in England and have recently got married). One of the phrases from the summer schools that has really stuck with me is this: 'Start with what's in your hand'. I think that that is what I'm doing. I'm currently looking for work and investigating courses to develop this call I feel to pioneer, but I'm starting with what's in my hand. My husband and I have made a conscious decision that we want our home to be a place of welcome and peace – a place where, hopefully, people can sense the presence of God. We're enjoying developing friendships and building relationships with those around us.

I'm excited about what the future holds. I don't know what that is, but I do know the One who calls me to follow him there, to the wild places – the One who teaches me to dance.

Siân Ashby

The reality and importance of taking risks has come across in the voices that we have heard. It is something we face, not just when choosing a specific action, but in looking at the culture of our group: are we risk-takers or are we risk averse? If our culture is risk averse, we will need to change this, for the dominance of a risk-averse culture will 'eat' any strategy to develop a fresh expression of church. If we are risk-takers, which we should be, how do we know the difference between appropriate risks and foolish ones? In Part 4, we'll look at risk and risk-taking in more detail.

Here we will leave our thoughts on sharing a vision by highlighting that, five years ago, we set out to help bring about a change of culture and outlook within our church – local, regional and national. The degree to which this change has taken place will profoundly affect the development, or otherwise, of fresh expressions of church within our denomination and, in turn, within the wider church. No church, never mind no person, is an island dislocated from the whole.

Notes

1 *Star Trek VII Generations.*

2 This theme of choosing between fantasy and reality, with all the attendant risks, is also a key theme of *The Matrix* (Warner Bros. 1999). When Neo, the central character of the film, makes his choice for reality rather than fantasy, he, like Kirk, will suffer, but he too will bring a form of salvation to others. Morpheus, who has offered him the choice, greets his transition with the words 'Welcome to the real world'. It's worth thinking about when we hear this phase used and by whom. Often it is used not in reference to fantasy and reality, but in reference to exposure to aspects of reality. Here we need to have discernment between a world where reality has been 'filtered' to effectively form a comforting fantasy and a world that is fully real, but more limited than another to certain aspects of life. So is the Westminster Bubble or the Ivory Tower necessarily less real than the Factory Floor? Or do they all need one another to understand reality better and avoid creating self-focused fantasies?

3 Tommy MacNeil, 'Releasing a Vision – Martin's Memorial and The Shed project', Stornoway, June 2018.

4 Colonel Thomas Edward Lawrence, *Seven Pillars of Wisdom* (Ware: Wordsworth Editions, 1997 [1927]) p. 7.

5 Hudson Taylor, quoted in *Our Daily Bread*, 16 May 1992. Source: www.sermonillustrations.com/a-z/p/provision.htm.

6 Michael Harvey, Chief Executive National Weekend of Invitation, 'Bringing Faith to our Imagination and Facing Fear', June 2018.

7 From a collection of essays by A.W. Tozer called *Born After Midnight* (Camp Hill, PA: Christian Publications, 1992 [1959]), pp. 94–5.

8 An interesting take on this question is an engineering joke, where the answer is another question, 'Why is it twice as big as it needs to be?' This is a useful reminder that not only do we need those who can appreciate something from a radically different angle, but also that we must not always allow the questioner to define the parameters of the answer.

9 Cole, Neil, *Organic Church: Growing Faith Where Life Happens*, 1st edition (San Francisco, CA: Jossey-Bass, 2005), p. 11.

10 Matthew 16:18.

11 In conversation with Lesley Hamilton-Messer, she recalled how, 'One of my lecturers at Cliff College was the Methodist minister and missionary Rev Prof Dr David Dunn-Wilson, and he spoke on "Why congregations fail to be missional." It should be noted that he spoke of the congregation as an entity which was more than the sum of its individual parts, and that discipling a congregation was more than teaching a series of individuals. The community dynamic was vital.

He spoke of the effects of a faulty catechism of holiness set against mission. In his view people who have sincerely tried to be faithful to the perceived call to be holy can easily become defensive when they feel berated for a lack of missional focus. The fault, he felt, was not theirs, but that of those who failed to appropriately disciple them (poor pastoring and teaching) – a lineage that sometimes went back generations. The question then is how do we gently rouse these folk to a missional awareness, without condemning them for the failing of others.'

12 Donovan, Vincent J., *Christianity Rediscovered* (Maryknoll, NY: Orbis Books, 1978).

13 Bowen, John P., '"What Happened Next?" Vincent Donovan, Thirty-Five Years On', *International Bulletin of Missionary Research*, 33:2, April 2009, pp. 79–82. Available online at www.international-bulletin.org/issues/2009-02/2009-02-079-bowen.html.

14 Often attributed to Peter Drucker.

15 *One Flew over the Cuckoo's Nest*, directed by Miloš Forman, United Artists, 1975.

16 In the context of fresh expressions of church, pioneering has the connotation of going out and settling for the sake of those who are 'out there', not for the pioneers or their particular community. However, in some cultural contexts the word can carry other associations, e.g. conquest, imperialism, the displacing of others.

Further, Pioneer is a generic term, which covers not only a range of temperament and calling, but should not be necessarily contrasted with settler. Pioneers go out and settle – they develop new communities; in this context, we find 'pioneer-settlers' as well as those who after their initial arriving will go out again.

It is also important to discern between those times when an individual or a community needs to be challenged to pioneer and those times when there needs to be a recognition of complementary gifts and calling and the affirmation of these.

17 Helen Brough, FORGE Scotland, 'Pioneer Leadership – more than a job title', June 2018.

18 https://en.oxforddictionaries.com/thesaurus/pioneer.

19 Barna Global, *Transforming Scotland: The State of Christianity, Faith and Church in Scotland* (Ventura, CA: Barna Group, 2015), p. 17.

20 A. Dalakoura, 'Differentiating Leader and Leadership Development', *Journal of Management Development*, 29:5, 2010, pp. 432–41.

21 A. Hirsch, *Forgotten Ways* (Ada, MI: Brazos Press, 2016), p. 209.

22 Over the three years, most presbyteries took up our 'Going for Growth' afternoon event invitation, although only a minority of local churches did so for the evening meeting; but in each case, it did give us a relational basis to build upon for Vision Days and other follow-up. The importance of the time between the initial Going for Growth events and the Vision Day, for communications and the developing of relationships, was highlighted by the higher representation of local churches at Vision

Days than at the Going for Growth evening events. Through these two sets of gatherings, an increasing awareness and understanding of fresh expressions of church has developed.

23 David Logue, 'Experience of Summer School', Argyll, May 2018.

24 Siân Ashby, 'Experience of Summer School', Peterborough, June 2018.

6

Getting Started

With contributions from Lesley Hamilton-Messer,
Norman Smith and Angus Mathieson.

In Tolkien's *The Fellowship of the Ring*,[1] there comes a point when Frodo realises that it is his responsibility to take the Ring to its destruction, in the Land of Mordor. He accepts this task while in the haven of Rivendell. In the film[2] of the book, as he is leaving this place of comfort, he hesitates and stops. He turns to Gandalf and asks, 'Mordor, Gandalf, is it left or right?'

At the early stages in the development of a fresh expression of church, many of us feel like Frodo: we are sure what we must do, but how do we get started? The three short contributions in this chapter help us take that initial step. They are personal reflections. Lesley, Norman and Angus write from their own experience; they write from what has been lived out; they help us 'earth' what we considered in the previous chapter: 'Sharing a Vision'.

There are many very helpful resources available on beginning a fresh expression of church;[3] we hope that our reflections, based on our experience in Scotland, complement these. Perhaps we are full of excitement and optimism, or perhaps if we are honest, we feel more like how Frodo and his companions must have felt as they left the warmth of Elrond's home and stood on the lonely moor:

> They crossed the bridge and wound slowly up the long, steep paths that led out of the cloven vale of Rivendell; and they came at length to the high moor where the wind hissed through the heather. Then with one glance at the Last Homely House twinkling below them they strode away far into the night.[4]

We begin with listening. Lesley Hamilton-Messer[5] moves us towards a deep honesty: about ourselves, the cost of listening and the life which it brings. When we embark on the adventure of fresh expressions of church, we intentionally give ourselves nowhere to hide.

Listening

The trouble with listening is that you don't know what you're going to hear until it's too late.

Even as a child, I had a real aversion to the phone – I just wouldn't use it. This persisted into adulthood, and I would be sweating at the thought of having to make a call, particularly to someone I didn't know well. Inconvenient in my personal life, this became pretty debilitating in the workplace, as I struggled to conceal my anxiety under the watchful eyes of my colleagues and manager.

Without the armour of either confidence or assertiveness, I imagined every encounter on the dreaded device as an opportunity to be abused or taken advantage of. However it had started, it had become a smokescreen for avoiding conversations that, if I'm honest, might demand more of me than I'd bargained for. Unfortunately, I wouldn't know that was going to happen until it was too late. Once I'd listened, I couldn't unhear what was said, and might finish the encounter feeling obligated and put upon.

Eventually the penny dropped, and I realised that the phone wasn't the issue. The medium wasn't what concerned me; it was the encounter with people. Once I admitted that, I saw other ways in which I avoided genuine conversations with people. I don't believe I was particularly selfish or uncaring; on the contrary, I was deeply interested in the people around me. The fault lay in believing real relationships could happen at arm's length. I behaved like a naturalist making field notes from the concealment of a hide – observing, but never interacting – rather than as a friend or neighbour.

With the dawning of my new self-awareness, I realised that despite the number of factors at work and different behaviours to overcome, the root cause was actually fear – fear of being vulnerable. I hope I can boast of some progress since then, but it has been a slow process, and is by no means complete.

I've indulged in personal reflection here, but working with congregations across the country, hoping to encourage and support them as they listen for mission, some of what I have encountered seems familiar. The dynamics of listening in congregations or leadership teams are not that different to the experience of individuals, and fear, while helpfully steering us clear of danger, can also deprive us of genuine connection, real relationships and transformational experiences.

When we listen for mission, it's a multifaceted activity, listening to God, each other, the wider church and the context that we are working in. In such a complex listening task, it's challenging to hold each thread in tension with the others, particularly over an extended period, or when you're feeling that no-one is listening to *you*. In any one of these exchanges, we can feel bruised, exhausted or frustrated, and begin to hold others at a distance to lessen the impact. In doing so, we can also deny ourselves and others an experience which is enriching, rewarding and transformative.

You see, the trouble with not listening is that you'll never know what you missed.

The fear of being vulnerable can make us long for safety, predictability and control. Rather than feeling engaged, we feel threatened by conversations that we don't already

know the outcome of. We fail to ask questions that we
don't have the answer to. But that predicable, controlled
state is not necessarily the safest place to be. The status
quo is not risk free – it just has dangers that we're familiar with.

If listening to our teams, congregations, communities or
God requires us to make changes, it might not be easy, but
it is necessary – growth doesn't happen without change.
Listening honours and values those we listen to. It shares
information and ideas and builds relationships. At its best,
it can provide a space for collaborative creativity that can
change our lives, communities and the world we live in.

I waited years for the confidence to arrive that would
make me a better listener. It didn't. What changed is that
I chose not to let my fear limit my life. Was it easy? – No.
Did it happen overnight? – No. Did I ever slip back into my
old habits? – Absolutely. Was it worth it? – Definitely.
What did that actually look like though? There were five
main areas where I chose to change my attitude.

Choosing to Be Honest

We're always hearing a certain amount of 'background noise'
that we take with us into any conversation. It might come
from our fears or ambitions. It may be a set of assumptions
that we have never challenged, or come from our culture
or context. Recognising these inner voices and giving them
their appropriate place in our considerations is far more
beneficial than denying or supressing our own thoughts and
feelings. Choosing to act in spite of our anxiety, tiredness or
frustration is not the same as denying we have any.

Choosing to Be Open-Minded

When we engage with others to gain approval for our pre-existing viewpoint, it is not really listening. Even when we are sure that our motives are the best, confirmation bias can stop us hearing what is actually being said. Even when our intentions are honest and we're not aware of doing this, there can be deep-seated assumptions, hopes or fears at play. The symptoms of deep listening can be uncomfortable, and if we repeatedly come away from an encounter having had no surprises, or felt no challenge, the chances are we're missing something important.

Choosing to Be Patient

The listening stage of mission takes time. It can't be rushed, and there really isn't a time to stop. The pressure to act, a sense of urgency or externally imposed deadlines and targets can tempt us to act too soon. It's worth the wait though. When we begin to listen, ideas can quickly start to form, but not everyone will come to the same conclusions or on the same timescale. It's tempting to get a project underway when the first idea presents itself, but take time to ponder it. Have we listened to all the stakeholders? Have we heard people's response? Have we waited on God?

Get this right – give the conversation time to ferment, give people time to gather and process information, and time to discern a course of action – and the rest follows much more easily. Rush it, and there's a greater risk of ending back at square one, having already expended a lot of time, resources and energy.

Choosing to Be Curious

When others challenge our plans or opinions, it can be tough. Our natural reaction is to become defensive, particularly if it involves something that's close to our heart, or something into which we have put a lot of time and energy. At that point, we usually stop listening and begin preparing our rebuttal. When I catch myself in the act of mentally gearing up to defend my position, I try to be curious instead – about others, about God and not least about myself. I ask 'why?' Why am I reacting this way? Why am I reluctant to hear that? Why does she want to do it that way? Why does that upset him so much? Why do we keep going round in circles?

Choosing to Be Generous

Listening is not something that comes without cost. It requires time and can take an emotional toll. When we listen for mission, if we genuinely want to hear God's plans for us in our current context, it might involve holding our own plans lightly. It requires resilience to understand that people can challenge our ideas while not challenging our character or sense of identity. In letting go of what we hold dear, we may actually free ourselves up to receive something even better.

This has been a small part of my journey – and I don't suggest that my experience is the same as that of others. As I move forward, I want to be someone with the courage to choose to listen more and listen better. I still struggle with my fears for the future, but I am also genuinely looking forward to what each encounter might bring, and to embrace, not avoid, the possibilities.

Lesley Hamilton-Messer

A well-known adage says that the longest journey begins with the first step, but with equal truth it has also been said that the longest journey begins from where you are.

Norman Smith[6] helps hold these two wisdoms together.

First Steps

Before being a minister, I worked as a painter and decorator. One of the things my boss ingrained in me was the need for preparation; if you want to do a good job, you don't start with a paintbrush. In fact, the more preparation you put in, the better the final job will be. I spent many hours learning the ropes of sanding, dusting, filling, sanding some more, priming, undercoating and top coating.

It's the same with Fresh Expressions, preparation is needed. Should you wake up one day with a burning desire to go and plant a fresh expression then consider the following.

Does the Congregation Understand What a Fresh Expression Is?

Typically, congregations are focused on their own activity and their own life. Much of our energy is designed to get people back into the church to become part of the existing community. Yet fresh expressions are about people going out and staying out. Do people in the church understand this will usually not result in more people coming to existing services?

How these kinds of expectations are managed is important to get right, which means that before doing any activity we should understand what it is that we are doing. Otherwise down the line problems arise such as, 'Why are we investing so much in people that don't even worship

---

with us?' Misplaced expectations can sour relations between existing churches and fresh expressions when there is no need for this to happen; if we prepare properly.

How Do We Help People Learn About Fresh Expressions?

Jean Piaget, the renowned psychologist, characterised two different ways in which people learn: Assimilation and Accommodation.

Assimilation is the easier one – where we fit a new piece of learning into existing thinking. If you see a new model of car come down the road, it might look different but it's still a car. It might be a hybrid or electric, yet the basic functionality remains that of a car, moving from point A to point B. You have effectively drawn on existing knowledge that helps you understand this is a different type of car.

Accommodation is more difficult. What would you do if the new car sprouted wings and took off? Is it a car, is it a plane, or a clane or a par? Here you must change the way you think to accommodate something new because it is beyond your current expectations. Yet when you do come to terms with the new thing, you really have expanded your horizons.

If you have read about fresh expressions or looked at their stories online or chatted about them with a friend, then you will already have an idea of what is involved. New information on fresh expressions will be easier for you to assimilate since you already have a point of reference. However, for those who have not travelled that road, it's a question of accommodating new thinking and that is going to take time.

Fresh expressions bring with them new ideas and new language, new practices and new expectations. For people raised in a particular style of church community who are comfortable with the existing way, asking them to adopt new ways should not be done quickly. While some people will pick things up swiftly, others will take longer and some will never accept church can be different to what they have experienced in their lives.

There are some basic approaches for helping people to understand fresh expressions. Gather a few people together and read a book. Follow that with a discussion over coffee where people can feel safe enough to really grapple with these new ideas. Go and visit an existing fresh expression where they can see how passionate those involved are to share the gospel. Keep up momentum by then running an MSI (Mission Shaped Initiative) or an MSM (Mission Shaped Ministry) course.[7] Above all, keep the conversation going, even when it's tough and people don't want to speak about this stuff.

You may think you are not getting anywhere, and you may become discouraged because you are not seeing anything happen. Remember though this is all about preparation. It is creating the fertile soil where new things can take root.

In the parable of the sower, we don't often ask, how was the fertile soil made fertile? What did the farmer do to make it fertile? Anyone who knows farming will tell you that keeping soil fertile actually takes a lot of work. You don't get a really good crop unless you first put the work in to keep the soil fertile.

But some seeds fell in good soil, and the plants bore grain: some had one hundred grains, others sixty, and others thirty. (Matthew 13:8; GNT)

From my own painting background, you don't get a really good finish unless you put lots of work into preparing at the start.

Where Do We Put That First Step?

One of the things I quickly learned in painting is that no two rooms are exactly the same. Placement of windows, doors, radiators and corners all had a bearing on where you started and where you finished. If you did try and do the same thing in different places, you soon found out what worked before was not going to work now. Before putting any wallpaper up or emulsion on any walls, it was critical to appraise each room on its own specific layout. You might call this painting in context.

Similarly, each and every situation we are called to witness in is different. We call this mission in context. What determines our first steps then is not the church from which we come and its expectations but the place we are going to work and its needs. That can be hard for churches who know what they want to see. It can be hard for the people who volunteer since they too will have expectations of what should happen.

Yet if we truly love the people we are called to serve, we will start where they are. How will we know what their needs are if we are not among them and how will we hear them if we do not listen to them? For a fresh expression to be effective, this principle of being among the people we are seeking to reach is non-negotiable. It is not therefore a question of acting on a community to make something happen but of being in the community, living as part of it. Every Christmas we celebrate the fact our God did this very thing when Jesus came as a child.

So having gained an understanding of fresh expressions, this must be accompanied by an understanding of our community. Only then will we be able to effectively relate the gospel in a meaningful way. All of which takes time.

Start at the beginning, with people. The more time you put into preparation, the better the outcome. It's worth going slowly at the start so you can take people with you and together you can see fresh expressions grow in your community.

Norman Smith

As we take our 'first steps', relationships will quite naturally begin to form. As these mature we expect the possibility of partnerships to open up and we intentionally and actively pursue their development. This is not always easy, and we have to be very careful not simply to move into the circle of those with whom we are most comfortable. Challenge is as important as affirmation, as is the valued companionship of not just 'the usual suspects'.

Angus Mathieson,[8] from his own journey, reminds us not only of the importance of this, but of how this has always been part of our best practice in being church.

Partnership for Me

Where I Started

Some thirty-seven years ago, a young Christian, aged 20, attended a large gathering of about 1,000 young people from all round the British Isles, camping on the Lincolnshire Agricultural Showground. It was an exhilarating experience, meeting with so many folk, sharing worship in those numbers. It was particularly so for someone from a small town of 8,000 people where everyone knew everyone else; a town whose identity had been forged in hard manual labour in pit and quarry, which was changing before his very eyes.

But what both those experiences – the big gathering and the small town – had in common is something that still resonates with the writer; for, Reader, I was that man. Being in community, whether en masse, or in the small town; or, for the purposes of this reflection, being in partnership, still lies at the heart of my faith and my work; my life and my discipleship.

My own faith journey, and my journey into ministry, has its roots in what used to be called the liberal wing of the church. I'm a member of the Iona Community,[9] and have been for over thirty years. The minister of the Church of Scotland congregation where I was nurtured had also been a member of the Iona Community, and he was a founding member of the Corrymeela Community.[10] He had also been heavily involved in the Charismatic Movement as a young minister. I think it was from him that I first learned to think outside the box and recognise that there was value in going outside any safe zone and working with partners, even if those partners weren't in the obvious places, and even if it's not easy – but nothing worthwhile is ever easy. I was pointed to a writer on social leadership, Julian Stodd, by a colleague – thank you Martin J. – and his blog has these words:

> To engage with those people we agree with is easy: to engage across dissent, hard. Within our tribes, our established social structures, we understand both power, and consequence, and can chart a safe path accordingly, but when we venture beyond our 'known' spaces, the risk is much higher.[11]

My time at theological college followed a year as an Iona Community Youth Volunteer, living in what today would be described as a new monastic community, with four members; I continued to be part of this small community for four years in all. There's a story to be written about that experiment, but here is not the place for it; but again partnerships were at the heart of our life together for that time.

Partnership Working in a Priority Area Parish

Nine years living and working as a community minister in what the Church of Scotland calls a Priority Area Parish reinforced that conviction in me. I spent much of those nine years experiencing significant change in local government, in particular watching swings between Labour and Conservative politics in succeeding general and local government elections, all of it impacting on daily life for myself and the other 9,000 folk living on the housing estates in that parish. Partnership working became second nature; working alongside members of the local community, local government officials, health agencies and politicians was challenging – but rewarding. Seeing a new clinic arise from the ashes of an all too small prefabricated bungalow made a difference – even if it was two years after the arguments had been won.

It's perhaps only now that I realise the value of the Poverty Truth Commission's slogan, 'Nothing About Us Without Us Is For Us', as being at the centre of what we were engaged in at that time. Being in partnership continues to be important for me.

Partnership Development Secretary and Beyond

I've worked in the offices of the Church of Scotland in George Street for over twenty years, and I'm heavily involved in a parish on the west side of Edinburgh, which does a great job of doing inherited church and which also does some exciting new work.

At the time of writing, I'm Secretary of the Church of Scotland's Mission and Discipleship Council, and I've been in this role for just over six months now. Before that however, I worked as Partnership Development Secretary for the Ministries Council; looking back, I wish the job had been called Partnerships Development Secretary, because I believe that the opportunities of being in partnership are integral to the mission of the church – including, but not limited to, the Church of Scotland. I also believe that there are any number of potential partners out there with whom the church can work.

Reflecting on my work as Partnership Development Secretary has been rewarding – and brings questions with it too. Working with my colleagues in other parts of the church to formally establish the relationship with Fresh Expressions UK; collaborating with others in establishing the Go For It fund[12] from three previous separate projects; and putting a funding package together for five ordained pioneer ministry posts, in radically different contexts,[13] from pioneering in the Farmers' Auction Market to the Artists' Studio and Installation,[14] are but a handful of those places where I've been privileged to work in partnership with others – and where others are invited into partnership with the one triune God.

I have enjoyed sharing in Fresh Expressions Vision Days in places as diverse as Shetland, Linlithgow, Dornoch and Glasgow, working with colleagues from Fresh Expressions UK, from the Methodist Church in Scotland and others in the Church of Scotland; and I have relished the opportunities offered by our formal partnership with Fresh

Expressions UK. At the time of writing, I hope to be in touch with my opposite numbers in one or two of the main UK denominations – and I'm willing to travel further . . . It was great listening to Steve Taylor from New Zealand earlier this year.[15]

I was ordained a Church of Scotland minister over thirty years ago, and I like to think that I've been open to different influences, to new partnerships, to new ways of being church and to being part of Going for Growth, mentioned above.[16] Going for Growth is no less than an attempt to move in hope, to talk about something that is worth sharing, worth doing, and getting away from the narrative of decline. The church in which I'm a minister today is a different church from the one into which I was ordained – but I still believe in its calling – to me, and its calling by God into mission.

What are the things I wish I'd learned earlier? That's a long story, more than this brief reflection will allow, but here are some ideas – few, if any, of which are original.

- Doing what we've always done will only result in the same; let's try out other possibilities, and who knows where the Spirit will lead.
- Those with whom we're comfortable may not be the people to show us new ways; God's Spirit works in many different ways and through many different agencies.
- Partnerships are challenging – and rewarding – but don't always work out. Perhaps we learn most when things don't go well . . .
- Culture change needs time and perseverance . . . but as someone else said, I love it when a plan comes together.
- Partnership working is relational – as is the Trinitarian nature of God.

Let the last words be with Julian Stodd:

> We will be unlikely to effect the change we wish to see if we operate purely within our known spaces: to truly change, we will have to engage in the hard ones. Engaging around our differences means bringing a certain humility, a certain strength, a willingness to share uncertainty. But if we can do so, if we can construct and share our stories of difference, then who knows, maybe we will truly change.[17]

Angus Mathieson

Notes

1 Tolkien, J. R. R., *The Lord of the Rings* (London: Allen and Unwin, 1954).

2 *The Fellowship of the Ring*, dir. Peter Jackson, New Line Cinema, 2001.

3 A good example is the 'Share' series of booklets, produced by Fresh Expressions UK, http://freshexpressions.org.uk, which help us work through each stage of a fresh expressions development. Another accessible resource is Michael Moynagh's book, *Being Church, Doing Life* (Oxford: Monarch Books, 2014).

4 Tolkien, J. R. R., *The Fellowship of the Ring* (London: Unwin Paperbacks, 1979), p. 367.

5 Lesley Hamilton-Messer, 'Listening', Edinburgh, June 2018.

6 Norman Smith, 'First Steps', Edinburgh, July 2018.

7 MSI (Mission Shaped Initiative) and MSM (Mission Shaped Ministry) are resources developed by Fresh Expressions (UK) to help groups and individuals understand better and think through the implications of fresh expressions of church in their local context.

8 Angus Mathieson, 'Partnership for me – where I started', Edinburgh, September 2018.

9 'The Iona Community is an ecumenical Christian community of women and men who seek to live out the Gospel in a way that is radical, inclusive and relevant to life in the 21st century . . . [it] is a dispersed Christian ecumenical community working for peace and social

justice, rebuilding of community and the renewal of worship.' Source: Iona Community website, https://iona.org.uk.

10 'Corrymeela is Northern Ireland's oldest peace and reconciliation organisation. We began before "The Troubles" and continue on in Northern Ireland's changing post-conflict society. The organisation grew organically from the original Community members, and today almost forty full-time staff and dozens of volunteers work alongside the eleven thousand people who spend time in our residential centre every year.

We are also a dispersed Christian Community . . . we are teachers, writers, people looking for work, retired people; we are young, middle-aged and old; we are people of doctrine and people of question. We are people who seek to engage with the differences of our world. We are people who disagree with each other on matters of religion, politics and economics. We are people who wish to name our own complicity in the fractures that damage our societies. We are people of dedication and commitment. We are people of prayers, conversation, curiosity and questioning. We are people of truth telling and hope. We are Corrymeela. And you are always welcome.' Source: Corrymeela website, www.corrymeela.org.

11 https://julianstodd.wordpress.com/2018/09/11/agreeing-to-disagree/, accessed 11 September 2018.

12 www.churchofscotland.org.uk/serve/go_for_it/about_the_fund, accessed 11 September 2018.

13 www.churchofscotland.org.uk/connect/going_for_growth, accessed 11 September 2018.

14 www.churchofscotland.org.uk/news_and_events/news/2018/ artist_rev_peter_gardner_hopes_to_bring_a_sense_of_peace_to_the_ general_assembly, accessed 11 September 2018.

15 www.emergentkiwi.org.nz/, accessed 11 September 2018.

16 www.churchofscotland.org.uk/connect/going_for_growth.

17 Julian Stodd, https://julianstodd.wordpress.com/2018/09/11/ agreeing-to-disagree/.

7

Discipleship

Discipleship is a term which we can use in referring to both 'being a disciple' and the 'making of disciples' and although the experience of being a disciple and discipling was a common reality in the world of Jesus, the term discipleship is not without its difficulties in our present world . . . it's important for us to be aware that for some discipleship can seem a hurdle. A hurdle not just in the sense that we all struggle with the integrity of our own living as bearers of Christ's name, but in the sense of fearing that discipleship and discipling is artificial to the relationships which we are building . . . churches and groups when thinking about the development of a fresh expression of church may easily see how listening, loving, serving and building community can develop, but somehow there seems a gulf between these and discipleship; somehow, for many, discipleship appears almost as an impertinent imposition, which we sneak in through the back door.

Earlier, in Chapter 1, when we noted the above, we made three basic points:

- First, 'we, as individuals and as a church community must always be open and honest about who we are. This is part of the integrity of the level playing field which we want to establish: we want everyone to move from the fear of pretence to the freedom of honesty. Our Christian identity may not be the first thing we share with a new acquaintance, that could be artificial; but, we should live out, wholeheartedly, who we are and, as such, express naturally our faith in word, thought and action.'

- Second, 'following from this we need to be confident that the Spirit of Jesus within us will be evident as we get on with the normal business of everyday life. The key is our wanting to be and to become the person and the community that Jesus wants us to be, despite our messing it up at times. If the Spirit of Jesus is within us that will be evident, we don't have to contrive this; we can relax.'
- Finally, 'when people encounter Jesus there is always the opportunity for change and transformation, even before a person may recognise who Jesus is. So, in a way, the formation of disciples may be happening from the very beginning, though it is likely to become more intentional as relationships and community develop.'

Before we develop these thoughts, some clarification may be helpful; clarification that comes from our searching, here in Scotland, for a deeper living out of our life with Jesus.

The first point to make relates to some of the difficulties we have with the term discipleship in our present context; this I know is not unique to us, but the following observations drawn from our experience may be helpful. Although in our general understanding within the church, discipleship has retained the elements of learning and following Jesus, this understanding has too often become mono-dimensional, 'flattened' and abstract. Too frequently, learning is seen as an intellectual exercise relating to facts; and behaviour is reduced to rules. Even the Bible is frequently understood as a book of rules to help us behave correctly, rather than a dynamic word of God, which centres on relationships; it is seen as a manual, rather than an intimate part of our conversation with God as we live and celebrate the most profound relationships in life.

This focus on the handing down of facts means that within churches discipleship is frequently centred on discipleship courses, which, in turn, often focus on the communication of information. Because of this misunderstanding, discipling and being a disciple has been distorted to the assimilation of the factual content of a good curriculum. We'll see later how the community of Hot Chocolate challenges this.

The second point follows on from this need to challenge mis-conceptions of discipleship and goes back to comments made earlier about what we have learnt about God. In the fresh expressions of church which I visit, there is a clear focus on 'being with': being with people and being with God. Discipleship, therefore, has a focus on being with Jesus and learning in this context. The theologian and writer Paula Gooder speaks of, 'Knocking about with Jesus',[1] not in a casual, whenever it suits sense, but with a wholehearted commitment to him through which we will be transformed.

Third, in the fresh expressions of church which we met in Part 2, we heard of both a seeking of God and of how God sees us and the community that we are serving. Paula Gooder's emphasis that, at the time of Jesus, core to being a disciple was not the learning of abstract facts or the transfer of ideas, but the transformation and understanding that come from see-ing the world through the eyes of the rabbi resonates deeply with our experience. Again and again, the people I interviewed spoke of seeing God, themselves and their communities in a whole new way; life had changed for them.

Fourth, often early on in the Gospel accounts, Jesus calls the disciples to both participate in the kingdom of God and to share in its proclamation. For many of us here in Scotland this is a real challenge as, for a variety of reasons, faith has become privatised. It is not that we hold back from lov-ing actions; our weakness is that we feel inadequate, fearful or lacking a right to give 'the reason for the hope' which we have.[2] As we have heard, from the fresh expressions of church which we have met in this book, participation, welcome, hospitality and a sharing with others are central to their way of life and are an essential part of the DNA which they pass on. This 'default' has the potential to give a healthy base for speaking about Jesus as we live and serve in his company.

Looking more widely than fresh expressions of church, the Mission and Discipleship Council of the Church of Scotland in its advocacy and resourcing of discipleship has highlighted the following six characteristics of discipleship:

1 Faith as a journey of discovery: How we listen to and learn from God as we seek to grow closer to God

2 Understanding who we are: Living life in all its fullness through understanding how God sees us and how God wants to use us

3 Whole-life worship: How we worship God with all our heart, soul and mind, both in times of worship and beyond

4 Prayer: How our journey of faith is shaped by listening to and conversing with God

5 Being a servant: How we go about loving our neighbour, inside and outside our church community

6 Discipling one another: How we shape others', and our own, faith journey through: being intentional about discipleship; sharing our faith; evangelising; connecting with those in our community; journeying with others.[3]

These characteristics give us a good base from which to explore four recurrent themes from our Scottish fresh expression of church experience.

- The breadth and depth of discipleship
- Apprenticeship and a culture of discipleship
- Intrinsic discipling
- The messiness of discipleship.

As we said in Chapter 1, when we think of the network of relationships that we have through Jesus, our relationship with the church 'universal' is a central one; and in the wider church the outworking of discipleship is a central theme. This has not only been true historically, but in our present time there is a fresh and intentional focus on this. This 'worldwide' perspective is crucial as discipleship is a communal as well as an individual experience; it has both an international and a local identity and dynamic. Our discipleship broadens and deepens as, together, we consciously walk with Jesus, learning with and from the local, national and international fellowship of the church.

In Tanzania, just over fifty miles south-west of Mount Kilimanjaro, lies the highland city of Arusha. A major tourist gateway to the world's highest free-standing mountain and to the 'endless' plains of the Serengeti, it is also a significant diplomatic hub – it hosted the International Criminal Tribunal for Rwanda.

Here in March 2018,[4] the World Council of Churches held a conference on World Mission and Evangelism; the theme was, 'Moving in the Spirit: Called to Transforming Discipleship'. Over 1,000 participants, all of whom were engaged in mission and evangelism, gathered from many different traditions and from every part of the world. The conference built upon the earlier 'Together Towards Life'[5] consultation and documentation, which explored the joy, challenge and urgency of mission and evangelism in our contemporary world and cultures. These conferences were nuanced to cultural differences and societal change, and they brought the richness of an international reflection to these themes.

As such, they gave breadth and depth, not just in their global spread, but in the holistic perspective of life, mission, evangelism and discipleship, which they stressed. The preparation and engagement was thorough, and after the Arusha Conference the following call was made to the worldwide church; an initial statement to explore and upon which to build.

We are called by our baptism to transforming discipleship: a Christ-connected way of life in a world where many face despair, rejection, loneliness, and worthlessness.

We are called to worship the one Triune God—the God of justice, love, and grace—at a time when many worship the false god of the market system (Luke 16:13).

We are called to proclaim the good news of Jesus Christ— the fullness of life, the repentance and forgiveness of sin, and the promise of eternal life—in word and deed, in a violent world where many are sacrificed to the idols of death (Jeremiah 32:35) and where many have not yet heard the gospel.

We are called to joyfully engage in the ways of the Holy Spirit, who empowers people from the margins with agency, in the search for justice and dignity (Acts 1:8; 4:31).

We are called to discern the word of God in a world that communicates many contradictory, false, and confusing messages.

We are called to care for God's creation, and to be in solidarity with nations severely affected by climate change in the face of a ruthless human-centred exploitation of the environment for consumerism and greed.

We are called as disciples to belong together in just and inclusive communities, in our quest for unity and on our ecumenical journey, in a world that is based upon marginalisation and exclusion.

We are called to be faithful witnesses of God's transforming love in dialogue with people of other faiths in a world where the politicisation of religious identities often causes conflict.

We are called to be formed as servant leaders who demonstrate the way of Christ in a world that privileges power, wealth, and the culture of money (Luke 22:25–7).

We are called to break down walls and seek justice with people who are dispossessed and displaced from their lands—including migrants, refugees and asylum seekers—and to resist new frontiers and borders that separate and kill (Isaiah 58:6–8).

We are called to follow the way of the cross, which challenges elitism, privilege, personal and structural power (Luke 9:23).

We are called to live in the light of the resurrection, which offers hope-filled possibilities for transformation.

This is a call to transforming discipleship.

This is not a call that we can answer in our own strength, so the call becomes, in the end, a call to prayer.[6]

One of the great gifts of the Arusha process is the engagement of the cross-cultural world church in helping a local church community deepen its discipleship. This universal involvement allows us to see through fresh eyes, avoid blind spots and gain new perspectives as together we be disciples and disciple one another.

In a more specific context, namely that of the UK, the scope of our understanding of discipleship has, in recent years, been brought under scrutiny. An important example of this is the work of the London Institute for Contemporary Christianity, which, with clear thinking and a pastoral heart, has challenged false perceptions and stunted frames of reference. They have championed a fresh embracing of discipleship as whole-life and life-long, where there is no secular/sacred divide in our understanding of the lordship of Jesus.[7]

What is notable about the various fresh expressions of church that I've encountered is that they seem to instinctively gravitate towards this rich understanding of discipleship. This is important as there is rightly the concern that a fresh expression of church, with its emphasis on listening to and serving a particular community, could end up as an 'all about me' church: it could encourage an individual and corporate self-centredness. However, the ethos of serving is so in the DNA of these churches that it seems to be readily inherited by those who engage with the community and are discipled by it.

I want to avoid a false idealism; all is not always rosy in the fresh expressions of church garden. Given our humanity and the ease with which we self-focus and self-deceive, problems, often painful ones, do arise; and the potential for this can increase as groups become more established and 'comfortable'. This is why an intrinsic part of the development of a fresh expression of church is the focus on mission, pioneering and moving out; including moving out from the new expression of church to establish a fresh expression in another context. This intentional understanding of being church and of discipleship is prevalent among fresh expressions of church; so, for example, as mentioned in Part 1, NYNO (Neither Young Nor Old) developed from Stockethill.

There is evident a present-day urgency in the worldwide church to grapple with and grasp the significance of discipleship in the deep, holistic living of everyday life. It is crucial that denominations and individual churches, whether inherited or fresh in expression, engage with and be part of this global ushering of God's Holy Spirit. We must listen to one another as we are open to the heart of God and to his daily call.

Language and culture are intimately linked in all sorts of ways. What we can express and how we express our understanding of the world are both aided and limited by the words which we speak. This is one of the reasons why active listening is so important; listening which safeguards us from interpreting the words of the other solely from our perspective and then fitting them into the world as we would most easily frame and understand it. We must listen with an openness of mind, heart and spirit, which allows us to first see and, as much as is possible, experience the world from the perspective of the one who is speaking. This does not necessarily imply agreement or collusion; it simply implies a mutual dignity, which leads to a greater understanding of reality and openness to appropriate change.

This listening to our culture, both in general and in particular contexts, helps us find the best words, metaphors and similes to express what we want to communicate; these will vary according to time and setting. The first-century reality of discipleship is no exception, and in certain contemporary contexts we need new images to help us understand its significance. All metaphors, models and similes have strengths, weaknesses and limitations, but one image, which seems to resonate with many today in fresh expressions of church, is that of 'Apprenticeship'.

Apprenticeship, where all are learners, has the connotation of a level playing field, yet a playing field where we can celebrate the different skills, abilities and experience that people bring to it. It also feeds in well to the present search for a 'culture of discipleship', which will focus on interdependent relationships of mutual support and accountability, rather than hierarchical pronouncements of prescriptive regulations. However, there is one important caveat, which we must make and stress, if we use this image: there can be only one Master Craftsperson; we will always be apprentices of Jesus and will always live in the ambience of mutual learning.

Jesus called his disciples to be like a child:[8] one, in their society, who was without rights and one who was completely dependent upon another. In our culture, with the recognition of the equal dignity and value of all (at least in theory) and the emphasis on protecting children and keeping them safe, it is hard for the force of Jesus' simile to make its appropriate impact. So, what simile, metaphor or image would help us today to hear what Jesus is saying?

One option is to see ourselves as stateless refugees on a packed boat on the Mediterranean Sea. We have our story, we have our dignity, we have our will and we have our identity, but we are dependent on the 'grace' of others for the shape of our future; we have no intrinsic security or capacity for independence. With this equality of dependence, we come, without pretence, into a community, a community where we will learn and where we will serve, a community which will expect humility and yet instil pride.

If we pursue the refugee imagery a little further, we can see that one former refugee, who has been granted citizenship of a community, can help a subsequent refugee who has just received this status. Yet the latter will have experiences and skills that can complement and help the former; there will be a mutuality of aim and of assistance. They both share the same goal – of integration into the new context – and they each want the best for the other and for others, who in time, they will get to know.

The 'culture of discipleship' that is growing in many fresh expressions of church is like this. There is the shared aim of genuinely wanting to be transformed by the Spirit of Jesus, to be the person and the community that God is calling us to be. Within this context, there is mutual assistance, love and accountability – not to dictate to the other, but to praise, comfort, challenge, share and show, to the other, what one considers to be the best way. The response is the responsibility of the other, though none in the community are indifferent to, or unaffected by, this response.

As we have said a number of times, church, and hence being a disciple, involves not only the particular and personal relationship that we have with Jesus, but also the rich matrix of relationships that we have in and through him. Discipleship is not the mere acquiring of knowledge; though, knowledge and understanding will have a part to play. Neither is it a programme; though, an intentional process may, at times, be involved. Discipleship is about 'being' a disciple, and it is profoundly relational. To help us earth this and see how a relational, interdependent apprenticeship model of discipleship might be lived out in practice, let's return to the community of Hot Chocolate.

The Hot Chocolate community is clear, not only about the centrality of relationships, for life, in general, but that the natural place, for a person to grow in faith and through which to share faith, is community. They are also very aware of our 'pervasive inclination to want to define, organise and control God and others'. They believe that the one who gets 'to define' is the one who 'makes meaning for the group',[9] and that the making of meaning is strongly related to power and control. So, as we've seen, listening, co-ownership and serving together are intentionally core to the identity and life of Hot Chocolate.

They see this relationship between defining, making meaning and holding power and control as particularly pertinent to discipleship. They, consciously, through others and through their own integrity, hold themselves to account regarding their motivation and practice; both in general and in discipleship.

We need to be honest about what we are doing and why. We can fool ourselves and think we are doing something for God, but in reality it is for us: our control and power . . . If we try to control God, we miss what he is doing even if we are wanting to be more discerning. All of us can deceive ourselves, so there is no room to point the finger.

The extent to which we stay in control, where people know the rules, leaves the power dynamics unexposed and unexplored, e.g. in exploring the Bible: if we stay in control of the message, it will 'bounce back'. However, if we are prepared to explore and allow our understanding to be vulnerable to the reaction of others – apathy, scorn, etc. – then we have a possibility to find something that will resonate with them, something more deeply truthful and embodied – more like the discipling of Jesus and Paul . . . Control of meaning is a key technique of abusers . . . What is important: Truth and Love, or Order and Staying in Control of our Reputation?[10]

Relating the above specifically to their understanding of discipleship,

We could do this [disciple] by asking what folk need to know and learn, and how, in turn, we could teach, transmit and deploy this. Hot Chocolate has a different starting point: we ask, 'How are we going to love this young person and enable them to become part of a community centred and shaped around God and his values?'

The first approach can identify important grounds of doctrine and practice, but the challenge and question is, 'Is this really relating to and affecting the other person?' The second approach has the strength of interaction and the building of a safe, honest community: a place where easy conversation happens. Depth and integrity is greater; what is harder is to guide this to cover key areas. Here we need to trust God to be the 'Course Director' re the curriculum, and we be the enablers and the sharers of life. Building a 'living in community' is much more difficult than finding organisational ways forward, but we get to what really matters for the person.[11]

For those in Hot Chocolate, discipleship is a natural process of life and this is what they want to reflect in their expression of church.

Person by person and step by step, through ups and downs, we are held by each other and God. We try to meet together, which explicitly and implicitly develops this mutual discipleship; this is slow. Hot Chocolate sees folk slowly and in small numbers go deeper in discipleship . . . Charles Gerkin stated that pastoral care is drawing out the story of where people are and God's story and 'blending the horizon'.

Praying together is one of the most important things we do together, though not a conventional approach . . . Prayer is simple, open and not controlled, e.g. 'Try Praying'[12] as a low-risk approach. People can step in and inhabit this space of prayer, even if they are uncertain about prayer.

In Hot Chocolate, this culture of discipleship allows each to be honest about their faith, doubts and questions. It allows an open apprenticeship that helps Christians avoid a self-protecting holding on to control, which can develop because of embarrassment or a lack of proper confidence.

Discipleship is slowed down for others when Christians are tentative about who they are and the centrality of their faith . . . Our lack of courage often holds us back. We feel self-conscious about being natural about our faith, and therefore we create a structure that gives us an advantage in the power dynamics and aids us in avoiding the 'curious conversation'. We do not need to privilege the gospel: be natural and let God be God.[13]

A common feature in the fresh expressions of church I meet is a culture of discipleship in which there is a mutual goal to encounter Jesus and be transformed by him, coupled with an agreed mutual accountability to be with one another during this transformation. This means that discipleship is not focused on prescribing certain actions, but on the integrity of the individual and the relationships of love and trust in the community; relationships that free each to comfort, challenge, offer guidance and ask for the same. It is not that actions are unimportant, they are; but, just as in being church, practice serves and flows from relationship, so it is with discipleship. As the Anglican Consultative Council has stated:

Discipleship is a God-ward transformation which takes place when individuals and community intentionally, sacrificially and consistently live every aspect of their daily life in commitment to following Jesus Christ.

It is a life-long, whole-life orientation, which will have challenging implications for our self-identity, our belonging within community, our belief systems and our daily behaviour.[14]

This concise statement, either directly or indirectly, helpfully draws attention to a number of core issues concerning discipleship. Some we have already mentioned, but two as yet we have not addressed.

The first is that the statement focuses on discipleship as 'intentional'. However, it is worth considering if some form of influencing or 'discipling' might take place before someone consciously becomes a disciple. Perhaps this seems an obscure point, but it isn't; it is important that we remember how we influence one another in everyday relationships. Each of us, by virtue of being part of society, is influenced and, in some way, shaped by others.

This influencing is at times deliberate. So, for example, various parties seek to influence our eating and drinking habits; they want us to see the world from their perspective, through their eyes. In a way, they are trying to disciple us along particular lines, lines that suit their goals, for example, health or profit. We may not have consciously signed up to these goals, but our interaction through media, or personal relationships, will affect us; we, consciously or unconsciously, may comply or resist. We are all affected by the ambience of a social pressure to conform.

However, as well as being influenced, each of us is, intrinsically, an influencer: our character, attitudes, values and actions have an effect on others. So, as we live our life in the wider community our intentional discipleship will affect others. This is not only through the influence of our words and actions, but, as we said in Chapter 1, because the Spirit of Jesus is 'within' us. People encounter the risen Christ in us, and when people encounter Jesus there is an opportunity for change and transformation.

We may prefer not to call this influencing and subsequent change discipleship, and reserve the term for an intentional attitude or openness; however, a shaping and significant change can take place by virtue of being in the company of another, or by sharing in a culture shaped by others. Whether we describe this as discipling or not is secondary; the important point is to recognise this intrinsic, mutual influencing.

However, before we leave this point, we should recognise that we have made an important assumption that has significant implications. We have assumed that from the very beginning, as we engage with a new community, we will have been upfront about living out our faith and, where appropriate, following Peter's earlier mentioned charge, 'Always be prepared to give an answer to everyone who asks you to give the reason for the hope that you have. But do this with gentleness and respect . . .' (1 Peter 3:15; NIV).

This integrity is crucial. It allows us to engage with others without any misunderstanding or pretence, and it frees us from misconstruing discipleship as something new, or even alien, which we bring into our developing relationships.

Over the years, I have been involved in pioneering two, what now would be termed, fresh expressions of church. The first was in a small town in the south of Spain and the second was in an urban priority area in the west of Scotland. On both occasions, we wanted to develop partnerships with community groups: statutory and voluntary. When we did this, we said two things: first, that we would never abuse the trust placed in us or the relationships that would develop; we would never use what we were doing in our partnership as a cover for proselytising. Second, and equally importantly, because we understood people in a holistic way with spiritual as well as physical, emotional, social and intellectual dimensions to their being, we would never shy away from being church and where appropriate addressing spiritual questions and needs. In neither context was there ever a problem as we lived out our discipleship. We influenced others and were influenced by them; we spoke of our faith, we discipled and were discipled. Of course, it wasn't always easy or straightforward, but there was no misunderstanding or perception of us being Machiavellian.

The second area, which we want to pick up from the Anglican Consultative Council statement, is slightly more complicated. The statement, understandably, expresses the ideal, not the messiness of discipleship. This is helpful, in that it keeps us focused on 'keeping the main thing, the main thing', but as life is more complex than ideals we must touch upon the intrinsic messiness and inconsistency of our discipleship and discipling.[15] Sean Stillman from Zac's Place comments that, 'Discipling is an incredibly messy business. It was messy for Jesus and it's messy for us.'[16]

To complicate things further, there is the issue of objectivity. How do we avoid a subjectivity that leads to a moral 'free for all'? In our mutual accountability, how do we know the direction to which we have committed to travel? How do we know when to affirm and when to challenge? What is the latitude for belief and practice? What is appropriate compromise?

In Part 2, when we looked at what we had learnt about our community, we highlighted the importance of the character of the kingdom of God and of the gospel in directing our action. I have found some words of Jesus in Matthew 19:8 incredibly helpful in applying this, and in discipleship and loving and serving others. There he implied that God, when guiding the people of Israel, could not always put his ideal into practice.[17] God had to take account of the waywardness of individuals and human society, yet be true to who he is. We can summarise what Jesus is commenting on here as 'principled' or 'virtuous' pragmatism; that is to say, God's action is both practical and guided by virtue.[18] We referred to this earlier in Chapter 5 when we spoke of our fear of compromising mission. This description of how God engages with the world opens a way for us through the tension which we might feel as we engage in mission and gives us a way of discerning what a proper compromise, when needed, might look like. It is an approach that can help us avoid getting lost or bogged down in a false idealism or purity, or being betrayed by an attractive utilitarianism. But, what does this phrase, 'principled' or 'virtuous' pragmatism, mean? We can only touch upon its implications here; but, three important areas for us to bear in mind are:

- First, when we think of 'principled' or 'virtuous' pragmatism, we are following our understanding of God and how he has expressed his love for us. The more I've thought about this, the more I realise that this isn't only in how God engages with us, in our imperfection, after the 'Fall', but also both in how he would relate to a perfect, pure creation (for example, before the 'Fall') and also how he will relate to a future 'new creation'. As creation is not the Creator, it inevitably has a limited capacity to experience and express the Divine, so, God must accommodate this in how he loves his creation. He must be pragmatic and accept a limitation of expression. However, this is a pragmatism that does not deny his nature and character; it is a pragmatism that expresses these in the very best way in this particular context. It seems to me that this is intrinsic to our understanding of the Creator/creature relationship, which we experience. This is reflected in the loving relationship of a parent to a small child, where the former cannot express all that is behind their actions, words and instructions. This does not imply an imperfection in the relationship; it only signifies that due to intrinsic levels of comprehension, experience and maturity there are appropriate limitations and foci of expression.[19]

  From Jesus' words in Matthew 19:8 we also see that 'principled' or 'virtuous' pragmatism was explicitly being worked out by God in the context of our 'fallen' world, and while this is not the place to develop further the significance of this theme in the pre-Christ story of Israel and earlier, I do believe that it is critical for our understanding of what was happening during this period with Israel and the world beyond it.[20]

- Second, when we look at the church as portrayed in the New Testament, we once again see the importance of 'principled' or 'virtuous' pragmatism; it helps us understand the bigger story of what was happening as well as specific aspects of mission. One example, which we referred to in Part 1 – The Council at Jerusalem[21] – is a good illustration of this. It is clear that, guided by the Holy Spirit, the church identified those principles, those ways of being, that reflected the heart of God and they centred their decision on these. So, the gentile church was not to be burdened by having to adhere to circumcision and the Law of Moses; there was no doubt about this. Yet, and it is an important yet, a behavioural 'burden' was put on the gentile church; one which the agreed principles theoretically freed them from.

> It seemed good to the Holy Spirit and to us not to burden you with anything beyond the following requirements. You will abstain from food sacrificed to idols, from blood, from the meat of strangled animals and from sexual immorality. You will do well to avoid these things. (Acts 15:28, 29, NIV)

This burden was a pragmatic one; it was not, theoretically, essential.[22] Its aim was, in practice, to help foster cross-cultural fellowship within the church. However, it was not a random utilitarianism: it was guided by principle and it allowed the church to live its life in the best way, as close to the ideal as possible, at this particular time and in this particular context. As with God and his love for us, the principle, the virtue, the good way of being is fundamental. It is from this basis that relationships and ways of relating are agreed; ways of living, which, in the reality of any particular context, are as close to the ideal as is possible.

- Third, in Chapter 5, we briefly mentioned John Bowen's thoughts on the work of the missionary Vincent Donovan. Bowen wondered,

> Maybe he [Donovan] could not have made the transition from pioneering to maintenance, from vision to reality: it seems not to have been his gift . . . [Others], however, were not the visionaries but the implementers of the vision. In the body of Christ, both are necessary.

If, for a moment, we link this to the writing of Alan Hirsch on apostles, prophets, evangelists, shepherds and teachers, we can see where principled, virtuous pragmatism is essential for the church today; in whatever expression. Alan Hirsch advocates that the five ministries mentioned in Ephesians 4 are essential for today's church. He comments that the first three have not had the profile of the latter two in the contemporary church, and he highlights the need for this imbalance to be redressed; without apostles, prophets and evangelists, mission will suffer. However, he does note that there can be a tension between the perspectives offered by the various callings.

Returning to John Bowen's comment on Vincent Donovan; I was recently in a group where Bowen's observation was seen as illustrating the tension between the vision of the prophet, with all the zeal and purity involved in this, and the pragmatism of the apostle, who wants to 'make it happen'. While this may be a, perhaps unfair, oversimplification and we may balk at this designation of role and perspective, it does give focus to what we're thinking about. In the present reality of our world, unless the purity of vision, which the prophet declares, is augmented by the earthedness and the relationships of the apostle, and of the shepherd, the vision, even if speaking truth, will lead us to falsehood. It will lead us to falsehood for, if there is not the proper compromise, it will call us to disengagement, isolation and abstraction, not an expressing of love in life and mission.

On the other hand, the vision of the prophet, as it expresses the heart of God, guides the action of the apostle, evangelist and shepherd. It clarifies purpose, guards integrity and helps ensure that message, messenger, words and action are coherent and resonate with the being and the love of God. Action is not based on the assumed amorality of 'what seems to work is best' or 'the end justifies the means', but on the foundation of who God is, on how God has made himself known to us and how we are called to be with God in each context.

So, 'principled' or 'virtuous pragmatism' is something that God has initiated and practises in his relating to us, and it gives us a way to best live out virtue in the reality of any particular context in which we live. However, if we are to have the wisdom and discernment to live this out in our daily life, it assumes a dependent openness to God and a conscious wanting to relate to him and understand who he is. Listening is also focal in this: to God, to the Other and to ourselves; we need to be open and honest about what is going on within us, our church and the wider community. If we come humbly before God and one another, the tensions that arise from different perspectives, experiences and gifts can, in reality, be helpful. We can begin to see these as a richness, rather than an irritation, and a more holistic and wholesome way forward can be understood and experienced.

In Scotland, we've had to apply a principled, virtuous pragmatism in a number of areas – areas which I suspect are familiar to many others. Decisions have had to be made about such things as celebration of the sacraments, governance, speed of change, timing of gatherings, the perception of competition and complementarity, the use and distribution of resources, the closing of groups (both inherited and fresh). Sometimes these decisions have been very constructive, and they have resonated strongly with the tone of the gathering in Jerusalem; at other times, a more painful parting of the ways has taken place.

Which brings us back to the wisdom of the closing words of the Arusha call to discipleship, wisdom that we ignore at great peril to ourselves and to others:

> This is not a call that we can answer in our own strength, so the call becomes, in the end, a call to prayer.[23]

Notes

1 Paula Gooder in a talk to Sheffield Diocese in 2015, available online at www.youtube.com/watch?v=EVq4LyxDKgo.

2 1 Peter 3:15.

3 Church of Scotland, Mission and Discipleship Council, November 2018.

4 Arusha, Tanzania, 8–13 March 2018. This conference was both preceded and followed up with very helpful discussion material. See World Council of Churches website, www.oikoumene.org, for this and for information on the prior Together Towards Life (September 2012) process and documentation: WCC Commission on World Mission and Evangelism Resources – Documentation. Also see footnote 14 for information on the Anglican community's present international engagement with Discipleship.

5 For further extensive reflection on 'Together Towards Life', see Ross, Kenneth R., Keum, Jooseop, Avtzi, Kyriaki and Hewitt, Roderick R. (eds), *Ecumenical Missiology: Changing Landscapes and New Conceptions of Mission* (Oxford: Regnum / Geneva: World Council of Churches 2016).

6 'Call to Discipleship' initial post-conference statement.

7 London Institute for Contemporary Christianity, www.licc.org. uk, see Whole-life Discipleship resources.

8 Matthew 18:1–4; 19:13–14.

9 Hot Chocolate interview. Here we are touching on a complex world of anthropology, psychology, social power, philosophy, theology and much more. The relationship of language, making meaning, power and control are graphically highlighted in Orwell, George, *1984* (London: Martin Secker and Warburg, 1949), as they are in the history of the church. For a theological and philosophical study of the use of language and our understanding of God, see Williams, Rowan, *The Edge of Words* (London: Bloomsbury, 2014): 'Our language claims, implicitly and explicitly, to present to us the patterns and rhythms of our environment – including the 'inner environment' of our own history or psychology – in a new form' (p. x).

10 Hot Chocolate interview.

11 Hot Chocolate interview.

12 'Try Praying' is a resource to sensitively encourage people to 'experiment' with prayer, www.trypraying.co.uk.

13 Hot Chocolate interview.

14 Anglican Consultative Council. Anglican Consultative Committee quoted in the Mission and Discipleship Council Report (Section 2.1) to the Church of Scotland General Assembly May 2018.

15 This statement, which was quoted in the Mission and Discipleship Council of the Church of Scotland report to the General Assembly 2018, should be read in the wider context of the Anglican Communion's current focus on discipleship, which engages with the complexity of discipleship. 'The current focus across the Anglican

Communion is on Intentional Discipleship which was the theme of the Anglican Consultative Council in 2016 (ACC-16). A Season of Intentional Discipleship and Disciple-Making (SIDD) was launched at ACC-16. It will run until ACC-19, in 2025.' (www.anglicancommunion. org/.../discipleship.aspx) See, for example, 'Intentional Discipleship and Disciple-Making: An Anglican Guide for Christian Life and Formation' (London: The Anglican Consultative Council, 2016).

16 Sean Stillman, 'Zac's Place' video, Fresh Expressions UK, http:// freshexpressions.org.uk.

17 It seems to me that as God knew that the ideal could not be implemented, the law that he gave to Moses expressed the closest realistic outworking of the ideal.

18 The term 'principled' may seem to some too impersonal, so 'virtuous' may be a better alternative as, in this context, it relates to the character of God and is the basis for any principle upon which we may act. Whichever term is preferred, the core idea is that:

- We must act, not just theorise.
- The ideal is not always possible.
- The end does not justify the means.
- All our actions are to be directed by that which is best, and they should approximate as closely as possible to this.

19 In *The Chronicles of Narnia*, by C. S. Lewis, Aslan relates to each of the characters as individuals. This reflects Jesus' words to Peter in John 21:20–2 and Revelation 2:17, 'To him who overcomes, I will give some of the hidden manna. I will also give him a white stone with a new name written on it, known only to him who receives it.' (NIV) This individuality and the relationship it entails will be reflected in not only how God engages with our gradual transformation in holiness, but also with our character, personality, interests, enthusiasms and our capacity to understand and express to others who God is.

This individuality is, given our limitations as creatures, essential so that corporately we may better express to one another, both within and outwith the church community, the wonder of God and so enrich the community of the church in worship and mission, and bless the wider community in witness.

20 This isn't the place to explore this theme further, but it helps us engage with areas such as God's relationship to the nature of Scripture, suffering and violence.

21 Acts 15:1–35.

22 See Stott, John, *The Message of Acts*, BST series (London: IVP, 1990), pp. 248–50 for a discussion on these requirements. The commentary on Acts 15:20 concludes that these requirements are ceremonial.

23 Arusha Call to Discipleship.

8

Parish Life

With contributions from Andrea Boyes, Liz Crumlish,
Peter Neilson and Albert Bogle.

When I heard the learn'd astronomer,
    When the proofs, the figures, were ranged in columns
before me,
    When I was shown the charts and diagrams, to add,
divide, and measure them,
    When I sitting heard the astronomer where he lectured
with much applause in the lecture-room,
    How soon unaccountable I became tired and sick;
    'Till rising and gliding out I wandered off by myself,
    In the mystical moist night-air, and from time to time,
    Looked up in perfect silence at the stars.
Walt Whitman[1]

Throughout this book, we've tried to focus, not on generalities
or abstract theory, but on what we, as a church, have learnt
through reflecting on our actual experience. Yet, for some, a
concern might remain: what might this mean in the everyday
realities of parish life? Like the character in Whitman's poem,
we may feel a serious discontent, unless we can ground all that
we have thought about in the realities of life, in its complexity
and fullness. While insight may be applauded, we will leave
its company if it winds along an isolated thread and does not
bring us closer to wholeness.

So, in this chapter, we want to focus on the dynamic of
parish life. As always, there is much more that could be said,
but this is a taster from the experience of practitioners as they

engage with mission and fresh expressions of church in a parish context.

In the Church of Scotland, the 5 per cent of parishes with the highest level of poverty, as indicated by the Scottish Indicators of Multiple Deprivation, are known as Priority Areas. These parishes are given specialised support, and it is from one of these that we hear. Andrea Boyes[2] picks up the story from when she arrived as parish minister in 2013.

Fresh Expressions of Church: Thoughts from a Parish Context

When asked what was the most important commandment, Jesus said: 'Love God and love your neighbours'. It's as if he is saying you cannot have one without the other.

Chalmers Church in Larkhall is a priority area charge set in the centre of a housing estate. I became the minister there in 2013. At that time, the church was part of the Church of Scotland's 'Chance to Thrive'[3] initiative for Priority Areas.

The 'Chance to Thrive' steering group was a supportive group of a few church members and elders, local volunteer organisations, head teachers, councillors and locals, all who were willing to offer their time, advice and skills, in partnership with the church's vision, to bring hope and renewal in our church and community. It was a group full of ideas, thoughts and lively discussion, wanting to seek a way forward, to grasp with issues that would bring thriving in an area with high deprivation.

There were challenging questions: of how to better support people to get online, access a computer to complete a job search and prevent being sanctioned; of how to support those who are elderly, isolated, lonely, homeless, have drug or alcohol addictions. How could we support children

---

in care, those with empty food cupboards and no electricity, or the children and young people who want something to do? How could we fund new initiatives, and how could we share the love of God in our community by loving our neighbours? How could we encourage the growth of both richness of skills and resilience of community? Yet, in and around all those questions was a heart for mission to share Christ and life in all its fullness.

As a new minister, I had been advised never to begin more than one new project in a year. However, as I gathered with the elders, met with the community, voluntary and statutory groups, and schools, it was clear that through these growing relationships something was happening. There was a willingness to come along on a fresh vision, a realisation that God had much more in store for us.

In the first few months of ministry, a small team was arranged to organise a community day in the church. Local voluntary groups connected to the parish were invited to have a stall to share their work, but no money was to be raised. There was entertainment by way of a local dance group, sumo suits and a bouncy castle. Worship in the sanctuary was full of enthusiastic Story Tellers, 'Out of the Box' puppets and children's squeals of laughter. I have several lasting images of that day: being amazed by over 500 people in and around the church, the laughter and joy in the busyness, a chap leaning on the wall at the back of the church smiling as he listened with his children to the story of the 'guid Samaritan' while sipping his can of beer, the real sense of hope that the church could reconnect with the community.

In the following weeks, a few of the elders and board members expressed their disappointment that out of all those people who had been at the community day, none had come to worship on the following Sundays. I had not grasped that some had held the hope that the community day would be the answer to church growth, particularly on a Sunday. There was some sharing and teaching still to be done, and the emphasis of this was upon mission – to engage or re-engage with the local community and the people, to connect, 'with people's culture, values, lifestyles and networks', where they are at.[4]

To engage with people is about understanding the context and story of those who are our neighbours; it is about being alongside them, in partnership, for the journey with Christ. Further, mission or 'evangelism in a post-modern environment needs to be love and truth in a dynamic partnership'.[5] To engage with people and help them take a step closer to Christ is first about churches asking, and then recognising, 'who is our neighbour?'; for Chalmers Church, this was the purpose of the community day; it was a first step in this process.

Over the next few years, the church began to grow, not numerically at first but in its missional outlook. The church grew in its discipleship as we leaned into where God would have us be. There were the first new initiatives – a Baby and Toddlers Group, a Tuesday Café, a Work Club, Tea Dances, a Craft Group – spaces to build relationships, spaces to share hospitality and welcome. As we served, we grew as disciples; we grew as we began to connect with an often-unchurched culture. As we connected and addressed issues, our discipleship deepened; it deepened because we were challenged to know why we believe and act as we do. I think in all of this we were, also, modelling discipleship to unchurched people because we were living out our lives around them in the Spirit of Jesus. As my friend Scott from Forge taught me, 'When people experience the love of God, genuine community and authentic spirituality, they become open to the message of Jesus'.

Three Wee Stories

Messy Church: After eight months in the church we began Messy Church. Relationships had been built and twenty to thirty people began to come along for the family church of crafts, games, lively worship and lunch. The helpers were all members of the traditional 'Sunday' church and a few raised questions as to, 'Why don't the families come on a Sunday?', or, 'How long do we support this?' The answer was that this was church – just a fresh expression of it.

I had some doubts as to whether those who came along to Messy Church really saw it as church, or their church, until one day in the supermarket I met a couple of mums. As we chatted, I spoke about Easter and a craft project we were doing in church. I asked if they would like to help and one mum asked, 'Is it our church?' I said, 'It's for Sunday', they both shook their heads and said, 'Nah! That's not our church. Our church is Messy Church.' The answer took me aback, but at the same time I was pleased to know they had found that genuine community; although we probably needed to think a bit more about how we shared the love of Jesus!

Messy Church was the beginning of a growing children and family ministry going on to employ children and family workers, who led Messy Church and much more.

Craft Group: This group started in the run-up to Christmas as we made crafts and thought a bit about how to manage Christmas on a budget. The women all thought it would be good to make this a regular group, and so we applied for a small grant. The majority of the women did not attend church, but every week, as we crafted and talked, I would be asked questions about church, God and faith. I asked the women if they would like to meet to talk more about these things. A friend had pointed me to a book called *Bad Girls of the Bible*, so Bad Girls began.

A fresh expression of church, where we met once the children had been dropped off at school, had a bacon roll and then opened our Bibles and read, discussed and discussed and discussed those bad girls of the Bible. Then we prayed. One woman with tears in her eyes said she had never been prayed for before and it was amazing. The bad girls had ups and downs, and there were weeks when the only bad girls there were the children and family worker and the minister.

Wheelie Church: The church building went through extensive renovations and outside was a very large car park. We had, over several summers, held indoor and outdoor skateboard and rollerblading days; this was with a local organisation, which had brought a mobile skate ramp and equipment. Alongside this, the school had contacted me, as pupils wanted to speak with me about helping to get a skate park or ramp in the local area. Also, there had been conversations with other leading members of the community, who offered help with funding.

At that time, due to the Glasgow Commonwealth Games, a funding application had become available for sporting activities. There was a growing momentum; so could we build a ramp in part of the church grounds? I spoke with our enthused 'Chance to Thrive' team and a property convener from presbytery; I put it past a general trustee and members of the community to see if there was any point in considering this further. All were positive.

Wheelie Church would be a church to connect with young people in an unchurched culture. I learned that skaters expressed their spirituality and feeling of something bigger when they were 'on it' (the skateboard that is). Wheelie Church was discussed with the elders and board; however, a small group brought great opposition, and the wheels came off. So, for the unity of the board, the project was dropped. Often, in ministry, it can feel like we have one leg in Christendom and the other in a postmodern world, trying to walk on unbalanced stilts, so it is good to pause, pray and listen.

Mission and beginning a fresh expression of Church is a real God-adventure of stepping out in faith. I have learned that to engage with others in the gospel, we have to let go of any fears we have of loving others; we have to question what fears we have that prevent us from loving others in the gospel. When we recognise these fears, we are able to move out. There is real freedom in this.

I've learned that being part of a team, or prayer team, is one way of being courageous and accountable as, together, you begin to prayerfully plan a fresh expression of church. Try not to be overly discouraged when others may not have the same vision, but be encouraged, in your discipleship, as you use and discover your gifts and the gifts of those you journey alongside. Go, make disciples!

Andrea Boyes

Weariness is a widespread reality in parish life. Often, those in leadership, in whatever form, are stretched to the limit (and at times beyond). Many times, I've been with folk who understand the vision of fresh expressions of church, but who feel that they, or their church community, simply don't have the capacity to do anything with this vision. We'll think more about this in Part 4, but at this point we want to consider 'Path of Renewal', an initiative within the Church of Scotland to help free up those in parish leadership, not only to dream, but also to begin to develop new forms of mission. These mission initiatives are not necessarily fresh expressions of church, but can include them. Liz Crumlish,[6] who has helped develop this initiative, writes:

Path of Renewal

Many congregations who once occupied a central place in their community, being built alongside or immediately after the housing stock that surrounds them, are, today, finding themselves on the margins. They are no longer regarded as a part of, or relevant to, the community they helped to form. Instead, their sad and neglected buildings, once a source of pride, serve as a reminder of a forgotten era, or as a place that one attends for a weight-loss class, or where one takes children for tap-dancing lessons.

The remnant of the faithful few, who still view this community facility as their place of worship, encumbered by the burden of keeping the roof intact and complying with a multitude of church and government regulations, have little energy to begin something new. But, many still have enough sense of purpose and vision to reimagine God's calling for them today.

Two years ago, I left a pastoral charge in the Church of Scotland to work on a project that seeks to transition congregations from maintenance to mission and from survival to flourishing. Through a network of residential training conferences, mentoring and learning communities, we seek to journey together, discovering God already at work in our communities and taking up God's invitation to join in. Support, collegiality and accountability are built in as we do theology together and as we respond to God's mission in our many different contexts. We are engaged in a movement not a programme.

The title of the project – Path of Renewal – comes from the work of William Bridges,[7] who describes the life cycle of organisations as involving various stages of growth and maturation. Bridges identifies a point at which the organisation or institution begins to close in on itself and must regenerate if it is to remain vital. He calls this process of regeneration the Path of Renewal.

This journey involves revisiting the dreaming and planning in which the institution invested in its early stages. For the church, that involves studying the journey of the people of God – from the relocation of Abraham to the journeying of the Israelites in the wilderness, from the settling in the Promised Land to the exile. It means revisiting the stories of the life of Jesus, the disciples and the early church to recover principles important to the mission of God; then adapting those principles to engage with the mission of God in our communities and culture today.

As a pilot project, it was important for us to work with congregations the length and breadth of Scotland, in rural and in urban areas and with differing demographics. We wanted to discover what factors might enhance or inhibit the growth that we hoped for. We deemed, however, that it was important that the congregations selected were led by those who saw the need for change and who had the gifts and skills to lead others through change, those who were committed to engaging in learning and reflecting on the changing nature of church life in the twenty-first century. These leaders needed to be able to identify those, particularly those on the fringes of church, with whom they might work collaboratively. In addition, from the outset, we asked for their commitment that once they had been through the process, they would mentor others through the same.

We used the image of the wildebeest, as we invited others to join us on a journey. Every year, wildebeest gather on the banks of the Mara River, waiting to cross to reach fertile plains and hunting and breeding grounds. They linger on the bank for weeks before crossing. No-one knows quite why or when, but, suddenly, one wildebeest will decide that it's time to cross and will leap into the predator-infested river. The amazing thing is that the other wildebeest do not wait until the first gets safely to the other side; they too leap into the water and take their chances, becoming part of a spectacular feat of nature as herds migrate.

In Path of Renewal, we asked folk to join us on a journey, a journey that involved risking the unknown, a journey through which we would support one another as we learned together how to discern the will and purpose of God for our lives and for the life of the church today.

From the beginning of the journey, together with over forty congregations we have learned and adapted along the way. This is an innovative and collaborative expedition that takes us off the map to engage in the mission of God.

Three essential elements of a missional church have underpinned the journey:

- Being involved in the community and beyond
- Creating authentic opportunities to form community and to worship together
- Nurturing faith at every age and stage of their lives.

At the beginning, we imagined that what was most needed was to encourage congregations to listen and become more involved in their communities. However, it soon became clear that the congregations with whom we were working were already pretty invested in that. That may in part be due to the fact that the Church of Scotland exercises a territorial ministry in every community in Scotland and has access to so many areas of community life – access that brings privilege and responsibility. Further, what we discovered was that, consistently, the most neglected of these three elements of missional church was nurturing

faith: discipleship. For so long, we have viewed church
membership as the end of the journey and not the beginning. And so, early in the process our focus moved to discipleship: how we can be disciples and how we can obey
Christ's commission to make disciples.

There has also been a focus on adaptive learning and
adaptive leadership. Finding ourselves at a point in the
history of the church when the many technical fixes in
which we invest simply serve to take us further along the
road of irrelevance – perfectly engineered to produce the
same results that have been ineffective for some time – we
are rediscovering the need for innovation and experimentation, both of which require a cultural change, a change
of heart and mind. Such change can be painful and often
involves loss. Skilful leadership, patience and compassion
are all required to accompany folk along this way of emotional turbulence.

From the outset, we focused on spiritual practices,
encouraging leaders to adopt a Rule of Life – a daily,
weekly and monthly calendar of spiritual practices that
would sustain them along the way as well as helping to
ground us in the word of God enabling us to discern more
fully the will and purpose of God for our lives and for the
life of the communities we serve. Each participant is held
accountable to their Rule of Life in their one-to-one mentoring and in their learning communities. It is important
that, as leaders, we develop, in the words of David Bosch,
a 'spirituality of the road'.[8]

Each year of the process, we have selected a particular
passage and journeyed with that passage, mining the deep
resources of Scripture in daily living.

Now in the third year of this project, having engaged
with over forty congregations, stories are emerging that
point to cultural change, a slow process.

One minister recently described some of the activities undertaken in his community, a traditional parish in urban Scotland, reporting that folk were smiling, talking, thinking, praying and caring more in church. People were more willing to give things a try, that young families were showing up and staying around; that folk were more appreciative of the community work done by church folk week in week out, seeing those varied activities as contributing to the well-being of the community.

There were also more folk asking questions and pondering their relationship with God and with each other. Having shared this, he was asked how this was any different to what had gone before. His response was to describe the cultural change that had taken place, citing a church now considered to be for the many, not for the few, a church that encourages wholesale participation, rather than restricted service for the in-crowd. A church that believes in its ability to make a difference in the community, being willing to risk and experiment and learn, participating in the mission of God and being willing to spend time discerning what that looks like in their community; new wine in old wine skins. Building the kingdom of God, rather than an extension to their church and discovering, along the way, freedom and excitement and the goodness of God.

In another congregation, a group of early adopters agreed to meet together to study Scripture, to pray, to encourage one another and to discern God's purpose for each of their lives. As they grew in confidence, they challenged and held each other accountable each week to bless their community. This led to each of them investing in two others, exploring and sharing their faith with them. Alongside this intentional discipleship, they took part in services, wrote in the church newsletter, initiated and encouraged a yarn bombing event in the community, and shared their involvement in Path of Renewal at every opportunity – so much so, that an elderly member of the congregation recently said: 'I'm still not entirely sure what Path of Renewal is but I can see the difference it has made in the lives of those involved'.

Path of Renewal has sought to foster relationship and collegiality among participants, promoting well-being and resilience as well as offering training and support previously unavailable in ministerial formation. This has been achieved through the educational input, the mentoring and learning communities, the encouragement of and accountability for spiritual practices and through forming and sustaining relationships rooted in prayer, theology and the awareness of journeying together into new territory. Theological differences have not prevented people working together positively through the process.

A further twenty-five congregations have joined the pilot, being mentored by those now in their third year of Path of Renewal. In this way, the movement should become sustainable and resource-light, making it more reproducible. As we work together with these new congregations, the lessons learned, the things discarded and discoveries made allow us to move forward, learning together, in all our different ministry contexts how God invites us to be involved in mission today. We do that valuing the treasures of the past, allowing these to inform the present, allowing all our stories to shape how we join in with God's story today and, together, forging a Path of Renewal shaped by the gospel today.

Liz Crumlish

A question that frequently arises is how a fresh expression of church can relate to an inherited expression of church in a parish context. Sometimes governance is in mind, but often, it is a more general concern: How can various expressions of church appreciate, support and encourage one another? How can they avoid misunderstanding and a rivalry for resources? Peter Neilson[9] offers the following model, one which we have found very helpful within the Church of Scotland.

The Parish as an Archipelago

A Missional Metaphor

Think of an archipelago of islands like the Orkney Islands, each island distinct yet recognised as a united identity called Orkney. That image of a parish community first came to mind when I was associate minister in the Parish Church of St Cuthbert in the centre of Edinburgh. This ancient congregation traces its roots back to Celtic times and is the mother church of many churches across Edinburgh.

I arrived there with the growing conviction that we needed to explore new patterns of church and to begin the conversation at the other end with people outwith the church. I had become convinced that having a church in every parish did not mean that every parish was churched. We need Christian communities in the neighbourhoods and networks of our increasingly fragmented society.

During my time with St Cuthbert's, we developed ministries in the business sector, the nightclub scene and among the homeless people of the streets. At times, it felt like visiting different islands of humanity, with very different life issues. In my mind's eye, I imagined rowing my boat from one island to the other in our parish archipelago.

Then I imagined the islands with the water drained away – a unified landmass with mountains that appeared above the water table. These islands share a common humanity whatever their social distinctives. Not only that, but they are all sustained by the colossal Christ of Colossians, the Christ 'in whom all things hold together' (Colossians 1:17).

Here was an image of profound unity that underpinned the superficial diversity. The traditional congregation was not 'the mainland' to which everyone was expected to travel – gathering in the one place at the one time to worship in the same way. It too was one of the islands. The church of Jesus Christ was the whole archipelago, one church in a range of forms, offering a variety of menu in a variety of venues.

A Mixed Economy

It was several years later that Rowan Williams floated the idea of a 'mixed economy' of church life where he described church as being wherever people gathered around the risen Christ in various places and forms.

If we strip away the usual fiscal application of the word 'economy', we are taken back to the Greek '*oikoumene*', meaning a 'household'. Within the household of God, there is room for diversity, while still being one family. The phrase has sometimes been replaced by the metaphor of a 'mixed ecology', recognising that different plants grow in different environments. That has some appeal given Jesus' many images of God's kingdom drawn from the natural world.

Many parishes are already an archipelago. We call them linkages and unions, or parish groupings or hubs, forged out of pragmatic necessity as circumstances change and staffing numbers fall. The different identities are usually determined by their history and represent, sadly, the management of decline. Their unity is defined in legal and constitutional terms rather than any theological, missional or relational basis.

Great Expectations

However, the Fresh Expressions approach to creating an archipelago parish is different, based on the missional intention of engaging people without a history of church involvement and with limited awareness of the Christian faith and life. The fresh expression may connect with a dormant spiritual search, particular needs to be met or gifts to be harnessed for the common good of the area.

As new 'island' communities emerge, a number of practical issues arise if the archipelago is to flourish.

Expectations may differ. Often the inherited congregation expects the new missional community to look like mother! Let me suggest a comparison. In the USA, there are calls for the church to address the deepening racial divisions. One African American professor at Princeton Seminary names the problem of 'the colour of whiteness',[10] the unspoken assumption that white is normal, natural and the controlling paradigm. In our churches, we have a problem with 'the colour of Christendom', smuggling in assumptions of what real church looks like. Other options are measured against it.

The parish as an archipelago depends on a profound mutual respect for the differing manifestations of Christian community, where neither new nor old looks down on the other. We cannot look up to those we look down on! This requires the humility of the mind of Christ revealed in his 'self-emptying' described by Paul in his letter to Philippi,[11] where each 'looks not only to his own interests, but also to the interests of others' (Philippians 2:4).

Expectations need realistic timelines. According to Hans Küng, every church is an 'interim church'[12] on a long journey to maturity. New churches are sometimes expected to deliver visible results in a short time. We need to think in decades rather than years. During the season of New Charge Developments in the Church of Scotland, a system of review was devised for years three, five, eight and ten, with a set of realistic expectations for each stage of the journey. That might be useful today.

Layered Oversight

As we have seen, the archipelago is not new. Malcolm Grundy[13] has written helpfully on 'multi-congregational ministry' and claims that the missing element has been intentional mission, due to inadequate oversight. He suggests that we need to 'watch over one another in community'. Some may say that is a good definition of the purpose of presbytery! Drawing on a wide range of Biblical and secular images of leadership, he distils the functions of oversight into three core themes: organic (listening, teaching, enabling), directional (interpreter, missioner, strategist, map-maker and navigator) and authoritative (guardian, reformer, legitimator, discipliner).

In emerging new churches, there is a strong organic emphasis on 'double listening' to the community and wider culture, and to the word and Spirit of God. They are usually led by people who can interpret the times, make the maps for mission and offer some navigation skills for the new journey.

The missing layer is the guardianship that protects from unhelpful institutional legal systems that are 'the colour of Christendom', but still provides the authorising environment for the new initiatives to flourish. In the Anglican world, a missionary bishop can provide that. In the Presbyterian world of the Church of Scotland, the nearest we come is the Presbytery Missionary Initiative, which does offer the permission within a defined legal framework.

Incubation and Innovation

In the Tollcross area of Edinburgh stands the large Baptist church known simply as Central. On a visit some time ago, I met two young women who were part of a missional community, part of Central, working in partnership with the Salvation Army among the street girls of Leith.

The story began in India where one of the young women, in a postgraduate year, had become aware of sex trafficking across Europe into UK, including our Scottish cities. When she returned to Scotland, she wanted to do something to help. The church had a group called 'incubate' where people with ideas for mission and outreach could meet and develop their ideas. At an evening service, she shared her vision and discovered a number of others who felt the same.

That group was then given support from the church leadership to develop a proper plan of action with an indication of costs and resources they needed to make it succeed. That plan was then presented to the leadership, approved as a missional community, and given the practical and prayerful support to bring it to fruition.

If you visit their website (www.centralchurch.co.uk), you will see this church has developed its own archipelago of over twenty communities serving the city of Edinburgh – an inspiring example for a parish church or a group of churches who are willing to release a matrix of ministries to serve our diverse communities.

It begins with a vision of God's kingdom that allows many visions and dreams to take root and flourish within that large vision, like a kaleidoscope of many colours.

But that is another metaphor for another time.

Peter Neilson

It is easy to recognise that for many, community is not organised around geographical location, but around interpersonal networks. However, since the 1990s these networks are increasingly not 'face-to-face', but 'virtual'. There is plenty of debate on the merits, or otherwise, of this; but, for our present focus, what is important is the reality of this feature of our world and how we may 'be' church in this exciting, vibrant context, which at times is uplifting, at other times toxic. What do listening, loving, serving and building community mean in this world of cyberspace? What is the affirmation and challenge of the kingdom of God, what is the particularly pertinent peace of the gospel for this immediate, yet distant world? How is discipleship deepened and church developed here, in a matrix, where pretence is easy and masks are custom made?

One fresh expression of church, which we have already met, directly engages with this dynamic. Sanctuary First is an online church, which engages with those whose 'home' is on the internet, but it does so in a way that is not exclusive, or isolationist. It interacts with the face-to-face and the geographical parish dynamic and seeks to integrate these with the cyber-world. It holds a holistic perspective. Albert Bogle[14] leads us through some of their thinking about online church in general and Sanctuary First in particular.

A New Faith Frontier

Online Church Challenges Outdated Boundaries

When we talk about 'online church', perhaps there is more 'on the line' than many of us want to acknowledge. Although some people fear the idea of faith being connected to technology as an innovation too far, the truth is technology has been used by the church to a greater or lesser extent for centuries. What is different today is the ability for almost everyone in the world to have instant communication with each other. This means that new kinds of community, centred around the internet, have grown up. The disturbing question, for church leaders, is, are we putting the future of traditional church communities, as we know them, 'on the line' or 'at risk' by developing alternative worshipping communities on the internet? I want to suggest that it may well be the internet that holds out a lifeline to the church, helping her to fulfil her Lord's command to go into all the world and communicate the gospel.

Opportunities Backed Up with Data

Local church leaders can be quite suspicious and even nervous about the validity of using technological innovation in worship. Often, this has come about because digital communication can be seen as frivolous and open to misuse and abuse. For some undoubtedly the internet can be a dangerous diversion, yet used positively, it can enhance our spiritual growth, not only at a personal level but, also, as worshipping communities. Nonetheless, questions continue to be asked of those who pioneer and promote the internet as a valid communication highway for the church. Sanctuary First seeks to answer these questions through monitoring the various pages on our site and using analytics to try and discover the usefulness of the material we commission.

Challenge to Vested Interests

Another reason why some are suspicious of growing the church online is because it challenges those who work to maintain church structures and central bureaucracies as they are at present. The internet offers a flat and more fluid structure for community and invites all to contribute. Those with vested interests who value control, regulation and order fear the organic, decentralised unpredictability of the internet. It offers a voice to the whole community, often rendering redundant the structures created by Victorian modernity and now inherited and promoted by some as godly tradition.

It allows for greater participation, but also calls for control to be relinquished or shared by another generation, a generation more familiar with the new communication technologies and more willing to be less doctrinaire, especially when it comes to structures and process.

Some of the above reasons may be why mainline Western churches struggle to see the significance of investing in this new wineskin. One thing is for certain, the old wineskin can no longer contain the new wine of a technological generation. For the first time ever according to data from digital analysts at GSMA Intelligence, there are more gadgets in the world than there are people, including a growing number that only communicate with other machines. The number of active mobile devices and human beings crossed over somewhere around the 7.19 billion mark. It is estimated by *Statistica* that 67 per cent of the world's population will own a mobile device by 2019. A recently published report by the Barna Group into how Christians in the USA are sharing their faith is described by them as follows:

> With the ubiquitous use of social media and mobile devices, the way we communicate has evolved—and, inevitably, so has the way we talk about faith. In a new report published in the USA in 2017, in partnership with Lutheran Hour Ministries, Barna asked American adults about how they discuss spirituality online. Through posts, comments and profiles, many Christians believe that technology and digital interactions have made evangelism easier: We found that three in 10 (28%) share their faith via social media, and almost six in 10 (58%) non-Christians say someone has shared their faith with them through Facebook.[15]

So, if you see someone in church looking at their phone during worship, be careful not to judge. Times are changing; they may well be following the Bible reading on their screen or taking notes on the sermon. (Perhaps the latter is a bit optimistic?) Though, they could be tweeting to a friend to 'tune in and log on' to the service, that is of course, if you are a church online. Perhaps we need to reassess the ubiquity of the internet. It need not be a departure or a distraction from our everyday lives – but an extension or a continuation of our present lives. The church should always be where life is – and the internet is increasingly where people are living. This means that the mainline churches need to catch up with where the people are. The internet is not a new place to go but a new tool to navigate the space we are already in.

Understanding the Ethos of 'Online Church'

When it comes to talking about 'church online' and 'online church', there is a distinction that needs to be made between these two approaches and to how they use the internet. Which way round we place the words determines how 'easy' or 'difficult' some of the questions will be when considering the relational, theological or ecclesial issues that surround internet expressions of church.

Church online is really church as you know it, only it uses the internet to communicate with its members and it might also 'live stream' the normal church service on a weekly basis to those not able to attend in person. Church online within a Scottish context remains rooted in a geographical area and by and large will keep a roll of membership, although in practice this may have little to do with pastoring the people and more to do with inherited tradition.

Online church is church that is completely centred and rooted to the internet. It has no building as such and may be less interested in roll keeping than finding ways to create interaction between those who frequent the site. St Pixels in the early noughties was the most famous of the online churches. It was 'Ship of Fools', a parachurch organisation in England, that explored this concept, defining themselves as a Christian community of people 'sharing their lives'. They developed a network of blogs, forums, chatroom events and offline meetings. St Pixels created a space for debate and questioning and has built its community around relationships that are about enquiry. In 2015, they transferred their operations over to Facebook, and it is from Facebook that they now seek to develop the idea of Christian community, by sharing their lives.

A New Model

Sanctuary First is seeking a new model of internet church. It has grown out of church online but now seeks an identity that is totally online, but not disconnected from geographically based church. In other words, we do not wish to be disconnected from geography, but neither do we wish to be defined by it. We want to be a bridge of renewal ready and open for the whole church to use, including our ecumenical partners.

This means we will challenge the idea that a worshipping community can only be geographically based. Sanctuary First, by its existence, brings into question the idea that only congregations living and working in secure geographical boundaries, and only serving those who live within these boundaries, can be recognised as valid worshipping communities of the Church of Scotland.

The internet cannot be restricted to a geographical area, just as God's Spirit cannot be restrained or contained in an area. This of course brings to the fore some of the issues mentioned earlier that surround what the church calls the provision of the 'ordinances of religion'.[16]

While the Church of Scotland understands the phrase 'bring the ordinances of religion to the people in every parish of Scotland through a territorial ministry' to mean a commitment to maintain worshipping, witnessing and serving Christian congregations throughout Scotland, the key part of the phrase is 'bringing the ordinances of religion to the people'. '[T]hrough a territorial ministry' is about a method of delivery, a method that suited a static, slow-moving society.

But that society is different now – it is faster and more fluid; people are defined less by geography than by digital technology, shortening distances and changing behaviour. Therefore, the church must be open to embracing new ways of 'bringing the ordinances of religion to the people'. The answer may well be through connectivity not geography – as a way of expanding, rather than replacing, the remit.

If someone is worshipping and being discipled daily by Sanctuary First, or an online congregation, surely this is fulfilling the role of a worshipping community? The question must then be asked, what should the rules be surrounding baptisms and weddings and pastoral care for those attached to online worshipping communities?

A New Highway

Sanctuary First is becoming the highway into a new faith frontier for the local church fulfilling the Great Commission by going out into all the world and at the same time offering the local church a road to liberation and freedom.

Sanctuary First would like to be in partnership with every congregation within the Church of Scotland. You might say we would like to be the online linked worshipping community for the whole church. We especially believe we can be of assistance to congregations who operate as church online and especially rural congregations, who operate out of two or three worshipping centres. It is these congregations who see their future as being church online, streaming the minister's sermon to the other centres simultaneously, while locally empowered elders lead the worship, introducing the hymns prayers and Scripture readings.

And where there is no minister, Sanctuary First can offer opportunities for live link-ups with other congregations who have a minister.

Sanctuary First as Resource to Church Online

Sanctuary First has already developed an extensive range of resources, which are at present helping to sustain and support congregations in rural and urban areas. Publishing original material, on a daily basis, that is relevant to the Scottish context means that more people are willing to use the material and engage with it. Our daily prayers and Bible reading attract thousands of daily worshippers.

During the past year, traffic on the site has increased 100 per cent. If we were to promote the traditional pastoral services of a worshipping community, it would be interesting to discover what the response might be. Offering the ordinances of religion via the internet may prove more effective and convenient for the worshipper. However, for presbyters who wish to keep to a strict geographical boundary, it may feel like an intrusion or a step too far. Finding opportunities to work in partnership with congregations is a model we seek to promote.

We continue to engage with our community on a regular basis through face-to-face events that are streamed out live on the internet. These occasions are highly valued especially by the users who cannot attend in person. During the season of Lent 2018, using questions relating to our daily Bible reading material, we set up four pilot Connect Groups to further explore the effectiveness of doing Bible study on the internet. This proved to be popular with those who attended. We believe there is an interest among Christian folk to meet informally, whether it be face-to-face or via Skype or FaceTime, to discuss issues arising from the Sanctuary First's daily reflections and Scripture readings.

Our ability to facilitate live streaming expertise for linked charges means that we bring a breadth of understanding and knowledge to congregations, allowing them to be more confident when seeking to explore their technological identity. In addition, there have been three Sanctuary First wedding services and at least two funeral services and enquiries have been received regarding baptisms. The latter requests were not possible, as a baptism in the Church of Scotland requires to be registered in a baptismal register, which is overseen by a kirk session. Sanctuary First operates at present without reference to a kirk session. However, even within present church law, there is no reason why Sanctuary First could not work in partnership with a kirk session to ensure a name is registered in the parish baptismal roll where the candidate lives.

The Disconnected Christian Diaspora

Steve Aisthorpe, in his book *The Invisible Church*,[17] highlights the growing number of Christians who no longer attend church regularly, but who still hold to their Christian faith. Sanctuary First is becoming the connection to reconnect some of these, known as the disconnected believers. Each week, we become aware of new people who fall into the above category. Finding us on the web, they are discovering our material helpful and inspiring. We are aware that some of these new connections are Christians who have, for whatever reason, stopped attending regular worship services.

Perhaps we are becoming a kind of third way. A community of believers made up of church online and online church in addition to offline churches. We have become a community, which because of our fluidity, is less defined. Yet, a community able to reach people and places where geographical church cannot go. A place where people can 'be' and become what they are called 'to be'.

We now prefer to call ourselves a worshipping community, rather than an online church. This gives us a freedom to embrace a wider concept of what it means to engage the people of God using the internet. It is more informal and sounds less institutionalised.

Conclusion

We believe we are uniquely placed to be one of a number of conduits for the renewal of the Church of Scotland, if the wider church can engage with the opportunities afforded by this fresh expression of church.

The rise of digital media allows the church to explore new ways to bring about a greater interaction with many who are sympathetic to Christianity, but who have become disconnected from the institution of traditional church. For many on the fringes of the church, Sanctuary First continues to be their choice of worshipping community, offering daily prayers and Bible readings that connect with the issues of their everyday lives.

We have become the Presbytery of Falkirk's fresh expression of church. If we are to grow and develop some of our ideas, we will require more staff and more resources. At present, we are in early conversations with three ministers in three different presbyteries, who are exploring with us and an interested funder the concept of a high street Sanctuary First cafe franchise. This would be a touching place where people, and especially parents and guardians of young children, can encounter the ethos of the Sanctuary Community, and of course eventually encounter the risen Christ for themselves.

We are also considering the changes that would be required if Sanctuary First were to become more inclusive and begin to engage with children and perhaps teenagers.[18] Our challenge is to remain a community that is both intergenerational and relevant to each age group. I guess it's the same challenge that faces every worshipping community.

It will be fascinating to see how presbyteries and councils of a geographically based church will, in future, reach out beyond their boundaries and use the internet to explore new frontiers. Building and sustaining new Christian faith fellowships on and off line must be one of the key priorities of local congregations. The new mantra is no longer church without walls, but parishes without boundaries.

Albert Bogle

Our companions in this section have helped us see how in practice fresh expressions of church can be earthed in the reality of parish life. They have encouraged us to realise that we really can be a part of this adventure, but they have not shied away from reminding us that disappointment (often profound) may also be ahead. Like all good adventure stories, we do not know what is round the corner; however, the big difference is that we know who is already there . . .

Notes

1 Walt Whitman, 'When I Heard the Learn'd Astronomer', in Untermeyer, Louis (ed.), *Albatross Book of Verse*, 3rd edition (London: Collins, 1968 [1960]), p. 439.

2 Andrea Boyes, 'Fresh Expressions of Church: thoughts from a parish perspective', June 2018.

3 'Chance to Thrive' is a Priority Areas' initiative supporting churches in their mission of engaging with the local community in ways that facilitate local aspirations for thriving. The programme encourages congregations to explore a 'Life, Space, Buildings' approach to mission and community thriving.

This begins by gaining an understanding of what life is like for people in the area, e.g. the good, the interests, the challenges, the enterprising and the connections. It then, second, wants to better appreciate how the community's environment impacts people's lives, e.g. by identifying the places of warmth and laughter, and those of shadow and avoidance. Third, the congregation is supported in a process of making its premises 'fit for purpose', manageable, sustainable and available as a community resource that facilitates thriving.

Chance to Thrive is committed to embedding an asset-based community development approach to its work.

4 Cray, Graham (ed.), *Mission-Shaped Church* (Norwich: Church House Publishing, 2004), p. 11.

5 Singlehurst, Laurence, *Cell Planting: Putting the 'Go' Back into Church* (Cel UK Training Series, 2009), p. 13.

6 Liz Crumlish, 'Path of Renewal', May 2018.

7 Bridges, William, *Managing Transition: Making the Most of Change* (Cambridge, MA: Da Capo Press, 2003), pp. 76–95.

8 Bosch, David J., *A Spirituality of the Road* (Scottdale, PA: Herald Press, 1979).

9 Peter Neilson, 'The Parish as an Archipelago', May 2018.

10 'The Colour of Whiteness' comes from a Leadership Webinar of that title in March 2018 by Dr Willie Jennings, Associate Professor of Systematic Theology and Africana Studies at Yale Divinity School. The webinar was under the auspices of Macedonian Ministry, an Atlanta-based organisation to support and encourage pastors.

11 Philippians 2:5–11.

12 Küng, Hans, *The Church* (London: Burns and Oates, 1968), p. 131.

13 Grundy, Malcolm, *Multi-Congregational Ministry: Theology and Practice for a Changing Church* (Norwich: Canterbury Press, 2015), pp. 86–99, 102.

14 Albert Bogle, 'A New Faith Frontier', June 2018.

15 *Spiritual Conversations in a Digital Age: How Christians' Approach to Sharing Their Faith Has Changed in 25 Years* (Ventura, CA: Barna Group, 2018).

16 See Appendix 3 for a note on the Church of Scotland and its structures; in particular, the note on the Articles Declaratory of the Constitution of the Church of Scotland.

17 Aisthorpe, Steve, *The Invisible Church* (Edinburgh: Saint Andrew Press, 2016), pp. 8, 201.

18 As we move forward to develop material and software, we will collaborate with the Church of Scotland's safeguarding unit to ensure that we develop models of good practice to ensure the safety of all in our community. Sanctuary First has at its heart a desire to be a safe place for all to explore faith.

Part 4

9

What Next?

One question that has become fundamental for us when we are introducing fresh expressions of church to a group, or when we are thinking and praying through how a venture is developing is, 'So what? What is the next step?' This isn't to encourage folk to make 'off the cuff' plans or in the enthusiasm of the moment to develop unrealistic schemes; it is to help ensure that we don't play games with the call of God.

We know from painful experience that it is all too easy to be enthused and glimpse a vision and then go away and let the run of life rob us of what we have received. Too easily, the weeds will sap the goodness of the soil and the briars will bar the path. Hence, we ask individuals and groups to take time to consider what God has been sharing with them; what has touched them and what must they now do with this? What is the next step?

This is likely to be a very small one, particularly if people are hearing about fresh expressions of church for the first time, but we ask them to decide what it might be. Then we ask them to think about how they will achieve it and how they will make themselves accountable in so doing. And this is what this last chapter is about: What is next for you? In hearing about some of our experiences in Scotland what has impressed you about God? How do you now see yourself, your church community and the wider community around you? What has God shared with you and what will you do with this?

To help us focus and begin to discern what this might be, we'll briefly re-emphasise three key themes at which we've already looked – the complexity of reality, motivation and listening – and then look at three others to which we have alluded – risk, weariness and gift.

There is a significant difference between simplifying a situation, so that our understanding may be deepened, and being simplistic. The former allows us to develop complexity, the latter negates the possibility. In 'HyperNormalisation',[1] Adam Curtis, the journalist and documentary maker, argues that the dominance and popular acceptance of simplistic, comfortable political and cultural explanations and strategies have left us incapable of engaging with the complexities of reality. Indeed, he goes further and claims that these simplistic explanations are built on falsehoods, but falsehoods that we can easily and reassuringly integrate into our false perception and understanding of the world. Here is an important wake-up call: life is complex, but we must avoid the simplistic and the false. How do we do this?

Core to our engaging with the complexity of life is our confidence and trust in God, and our listening to him. True, as we saw when we looked at 'principled' or 'virtuous' pragmatism, God cannot communicate everything to us, but the simplification that God gives us leads us deeper into truth. We will never see the whole picture, but the view to the horizon is God's gift to us. Yes, at times, a mist may fall, but we know what is there, even if unseen; and, to pursue the metaphor a little, as we move towards the horizon, we will see further.

To engage with the complexity of reality means to hold as provisional, or tentative, much of what we, at present, assume to be accurate. In his book *Sapiens*,[2] Yuval Noah Harari comments on the importance of the admission of ignorance for our capacity to progress. However, our readiness to be blinkered is such that we cannot take for granted our openness to engage with uncomfortable truths. An example from a pivotal point in the history of science illustrates this well.

Let's travel back over 400 years to a winter night in northern Italy: it is 7 January by the new calendar, the year is 1610 and we are in the town of Padua. Our companion is a teacher at the local university. His work is uncomfortable, but he is determined. He is one of the first to turn the newly invented 'spyglass' from day-lit earth to darkened sky, and on this night he witnesses a dance in space that will help challenge millennia of understanding. The planet Jupiter is not alone: other bodies circle it. This and his other observations convince him, Galileo Galilei, that the Earth circles the Sun and not the other way round. Imagine his excitement at catching this vision and then the gradual dawning of the challenge of convincing others to face the facts. His insight was not to be met with open arms: voices in science, philosophy, theology and the politics of church would caution and chastise him.

Now if, on this famous January night, we were to travel 400 miles north to the Bavarian town of Ansbach we would meet Simon Marius. Not as famous as Galileo, but he too is observing this celestial circling. Some of his observations are more refined than Galileo's, yet from this and his wider work he comes to a different conclusion about the order of the universe, namely that there are bodies which orbit Jupiter and Jupiter, in turn, orbits the Sun, but the Sun orbits the Earth. The universe is centred on the Earth.

Let's think for a moment about what is happening here, as this is a complex context into which our two companions have brought us. As we have said, while it is important to be able to simplify a situation, it is a different matter to be simplistic or to be content with caricatures. So, as has too often been the case, it would be easy to reduce this piece of history to a story of Galileo, the innovative, heroic pioneer standing up for truth against a tyrannical, obscurantist church protecting its dominance, power and prestige. Now, while there may be elements of truth in this caricature, it essentially incapacitates us and blinds us to the truth: the truth of a complex world where the influence of Aristotle's thinking about the structure of reality held sway, not just in the church, but in the culture as a whole. Voices scientific as well as ecclesial spoke out against Galileo's perspective in a world where power, personal rivalries, vanities and fears entered the melee and confused the protagonists' purity of motive. Even Marius did not 'see' where his observations and the accruing evidence were pointing. As is so often in life, we cannot point a finger. Rather, we need to ask, 'What

fears and prejudices, vanities and arrogance blind us and hold
sway? What unquestioned assumptions are given sovereignty
in our life? What perceived treasure do we need to let go, if we
are to be unburdened and free to step deeper into that which
is real?'

The second theme that we want to re-emphasise is motivation. We have already looked at this in some depth, so here
let's simply remember some words of John.

Dear friends, let us love one another, for love comes from
God. Everyone who loves has been born of God and knows
God. Whoever does not love does not know God, because
God is Love . . . Since God so loved us, we also ought to love
one another. No one has ever seen God, but if we love one
another, God lives in us and his love is made complete in us.
We know that we live in him and he in us, because he has
given us his Spirit . . . God is love. Whoever lives in love lives
in God and God in him. In this way love is made complete
among us . . . There is no fear in love. But perfect love drives
out fear . . . We love because he first loved us. If anyone says.
'I love God,' yet hates his brother, whom he has seen, he is a
liar. For anyone who does not love his brother, whom he has
seen, cannot love God, whom he has not seen. And he has
given us this command: Whoever loves God must also love
his brother. (1 John 4:7–21; NIV)

'Not much arguing with this', as they say . . . but, what does it
mean for your next step?

The final point to reiterate is listening. Here let's merely
emphasise that we are not only listening for the present,
but also for the future. This listening for the future has two
aspects. The first is, using a different sense metaphor, catching
a glimpse of the future and then shaping our actions in the light
of this.

Otto Scharmer and Katrin Kaufer entitled their book on transforming business, society and self, *Leading from the Emerging
Future*.[3] They argued that effective solutions for present challenges would not be found in past modes of thinking, but

through a sensing of what is emerging, or what wants to emerge. They based this on Scharmer's Theory U,[4] which has similarities to aspects of the process we looked at in Part 1, when we considered the development of fresh expressions of churches.

They stress the necessity to first open our minds, hearts and wills as we totally immerse ourselves in the places that matter most to the situation with which we are dealing. And then to retreat, reflect and allow an inner knowing to emerge; ask questions such as, 'What wants to emerge here?' 'How does that relate to the journey forward?' 'How can we become part of the story of the future rather than holding on to the story of the past?'

This is followed by exploring the future through doing.[5] Interestingly, their book is subtitled, 'From Ego-system to Eco-system', and they emphasise the need to move from obsolete systems focused on the well-being of oneself to a system that emphasises the well-being of the whole. While the philosophical influences that helped shape Theory U may not be those that have shaped the present developments of fresh expressions of church, there is a lot to glean from Scharmer and Kaufer's insights.

So it is, as we immerse ourselves in the new context in which we have been called to serve. As we humbly and actively listen, and as we then reflect together, in the presence of God, on what we hear, we get a sense not only of the next step, but perhaps, also, of the shape of things to come. However, in saying this, we need to be very careful about our expectations (remember what we said earlier about our intrinsic limitations); we are likely to have no clarity about the detail of what is emerging (that is the usual experience at this stage), but what we may well have is a sense of its qualities and character.

This understanding, which may arise from our engagement with the local, is complemented by our engagement with and our listening to the 'big picture'. In his Afternow project,[6] Phil Hanlon (Emeritus Professor of Public Health, Glasgow University) challenges us to understand our present time not just as an Age of Change, but as the liminal time before a Change of Age.[7] If this is so, how might this influence our next step?

The second way that we listen for the future follows from the first: we want to serve those in the future, so we listen on their behalf. What we begin to shape now is not just for the present, but also for what might be emerging in our culture(s). How we live now and how we enable ourselves and others to be church affect not only the here and now, but also the future. What 'baton' are we passing on? What future culture for church and mission have we helped shape?

Going back to the story of Galileo and Simon Marius, they both made incredible observations, but neither of them invented the telescope. The sighting of circling moons, with all that developed from the observing of this celestial dance, was built upon the ingenuity, wisdom and acumen of others; they were heirs who in turn left an inheritance. So too are we.

Now we come to the three themes to which we've alluded directly or indirectly. The first is one that we mentioned in our thinking in Chapter 5 about sharing a vision: risk. The reality and importance of risk and mission has come across in the voices that we have heard throughout this book. It is something that has been highlighted, not just when reflecting upon specific actions, but also when considering the culture of a group: are we risk-takers or are we risk averse? The opinion of the fresh expressions of church which we met is that we should be risk-takers, for God is a risk-taker.[8] However, if we accept that we should be risk-takers and that the culture of our churches and groups should be one of risk-taking, there arise crucial considerations and questions with which we must actively engage. Of these, we will mention only three: personality, perceived failure and appropriate risk.

Whether we give little or much credence to personality tests it cannot be denied that people can react differently to the same situation; this reaction may be due to experience, mood or something more intrinsic. For the sake of argument, let's call the latter personality and, for the point we want to emphasise, let's set aside the cultivation of character. Depending on our personality, we may react differently to order and disorder, the scripted and the improvised, the quiet and the noisy, solitude and crowd. There is no right and wrong in this (though, of course, there may be in how we express our reaction), there is merely legitimate difference. If most groups will, to some extent, contain a variety of personalities, then most church communities should expect an initial variation of reaction to the suggestion of pioneering a fresh expression of church – a variation not necessarily due to a weighing up of vision and risks, but due to something much more visceral and intrinsic to each person.

What is really important is not just our initial reaction, but the context in which we interpret and engage with this reaction. Is the context one of appreciation of others, openness to vision and mission, and a willingness to sacrifice and not insist on one's own preferences? Love, trust, appreciation, patience and good communication are essential as we take account of, benefit from and help one another with the different reactions due to our personality.

As we've thought about our experience here in Scotland, we've wanted to hold together vision and context, the ideal and the 'on the ground' reality. We've looked at the stories of groups that have seen, at least to some extent, their initial vision and hopes realised, but this has not been the case for everyone. For some, cherished dreams faded and disappeared in the harsh light of day.

'Dread of error is death of progress', words scrawled in crayon on the study wall of a professor I knew when I was a student. He enjoyed being a bit eccentric. But I still remember the impact that those words made when I first read them: words that gave permission to take risks when journeying in an honourable direction; words that called for a trusting openness to others, allowing them to point out my mistakes; words that demanded a deep honesty that freed me to be able to admit to getting it wrong or to realise that my dream was nothing but that. They are words, which, now I see, resonate with the adventure and experimentation of fresh expressions of church.

However, before we embark on an initiative, it is relatively easy to be open to the possibility of it not working out. It is often much more difficult, requiring much courage, to admit this a few years down the line, after we have invested so much.

How do we feel when this happens: about God, others and our-selves? How do we handle our emotions of disappointment, hurt, anger, relief, guilt, disillusionment? How do we face others who had previously been encouraged by our story and who had expected much from us? These things can go very deep; when they do, 'dread of error is death of progress' may seem glib, one-dimensional and mocking of our darkness and pain.

So, when we talk about risk, when we ask others to take risks and when we take risks, there are deep pastoral implications – implications which all too easily we can ignore. In general, we find it easier to seek out the company of those who seem to be making a difference, rather than walk a long, often unheralded, path with the crestfallen or disillusioned. But if we are to take the advocacy of fresh expressions of church seriously, then we must see the provision of fully comprehensive pastoral care as intrinsically non-negotiable. This is particularly the case for those who send others and support new ventures – be they local, regional or national.

While something may flounder due to our foolishness, disobedience to God or pride, that is not what we are thinking about here. Here we are thinking about something that is developed and carried through in an appropriate, constructive way, yet does not grow into what we had hoped. Perhaps in spite of our enthusiasm, effort and even great sacrifice, it never germinates or flourishes. An important question is: 'Is this really failure, or something that may be wrongly perceived as failure?' I think that the latter is the case. I say this, not to falsely ease a pain or to provide a way to 'save face', but because of the intrinsic nature of what we are involved in when we are developing a fresh expression of church.

A few years ago, in a discussion, Michael Moynagh[9] reminded us about the care we need to take with the language we use when we are speaking about fresh expression initiatives. One example we talked about was the use of the word 'Pilot'. This word can be helpful; however, it generally brings with it the connotation of success or failure. If the pilot goes according to plan, we will develop on this; if not, we will, with disappointment, try to learn from its failure. In regard to a fresh expression of church, there are two significant weaknesses with this frame of reference. First, it implies that we have a reasonably clear idea of how things should develop. Second, we set ourselves up for potential 'failure'.

However, what if we were to think in terms of an experiment? Again, there are dangers with this word as it can bring with it the association of being unengaged, distant, clinical and project-based; it can remove us from the relational, which is at the heart of a fresh expression of church, and all that is associated with it. That said, if we can see ourselves, along with all others involved, as active participants in a relational social experiment, then we can give ourselves a framework where, legitimately, failure is not a possible end result.

In an experiment, there are basically three possible outcomes: the results may be along the lines that we expected, or nothing may happen, or something totally unexpected may happen. Each result is a success, even the one where nothing happened. Provided we learn, deepen our understanding and act upon the results, the experiment will be successful in moving us forward; it will only be 'failure' if we choose not to respond in this way.

If we apply this to our thinking about fresh expressions of church, then even where we are profoundly disappointed with how relationships, community and church have failed to develop, we are not necessarily experiencing failure. If we, or others, can build on our experience, then our venture has brought success. Yet, in saying this, I'm aware of situations where there has been great pain and I realise that some may feel angry with what I'm saying. Understandably, they may see this as insensitive, theoretical whitewash, which adds to their hurt. However, from a perspective of experiment, let's think of God's action in creation and our subsequent 'Fall': it didn't work out as it should, we moved from life towards death, yet God built upon this – albeit at an unimaginable cost.

Even so, it may be very difficult to see a rainbow of hope. Perhaps the following may help:

- Never cease to be honest: don't lie or pretend with God, yourself and those who are with you on this journey.

- Remember that we are part of a big story and from almost the beginning, the sorrow of the garden tainted the joy of creation. Humankind's act of spitting in the face of love brought death to the one who loved.
- Remember how Jesus travelled, spoke, healed, experienced rejection and vitriol, and wept. How, in another garden, he pleaded with the Father for another way.
- Remember how Paul, led by the Spirit, eyeballed dark despair, yet experienced the grace to move forward; the weaving of grace and our reaction and the reactions of others to it, does not follow a simple pattern.
- When we are hurt, disillusioned and feel betrayed, we can be tempted to back away from others and from God. While at times it may be necessary to separate ourselves from those who harm us, we must be careful that we don't distance ourselves from the One and the ones who can help us. Our stepping back from them may be because we want to work it through on our own and then come back to them, or because we feel too vulnerable to have anyone near us. But we must avoid this temptation. When Jerusalem was surrounded by the Assyrian army of Sennacherib, what did Hezekiah do?[10] He took the letter of threat from Sennacherib, brought it to the temple, opened it before God and 'told it as it was'. Then he 'worked it through' with God, not on his own.
- We need people who will stay alongside us when the worst happens: those who will walk a long path and not just turn off at the next fork in the road and leave us alone with our grief.
- Remember what we, in easier times, have said to others about love, grace and worth. Are we loved because of our 'success'? Does this define us? No, these things are dependent on something much deeper.
- Remember that although we may be the victim of something, we must not define ourselves as victims; we should not understand our identity in terms of what has been done to us. Let us be shaped by our response to what we have experienced, not the experience itself.

This brings us to the third of our considerations concerning risk: how do we know the difference between an appropriate and an inappropriate risk? Essentially, this wisdom will come from understanding the motivation behind the action, not the action itself. An example might help . . .

In the 1980s during the 'Troubles' in Northern Ireland, the murder of 'random' citizens was not uncommon. As communities were segregated geographically, a group of terrorists could drive into a street of the other community and be more or less certain that anyone they would randomly shoot would be from this other community. At times during this period, it was unsafe to walk along certain streets, especially after dark.

I was working as an assistant parish minister in one of these areas; I knew that it would be utterly foolish to arbitrarily walk down particular streets in the parish at certain times. This would be an inappropriate risk. Yet, when I would receive a call at night to give urgent pastoral support to someone in one of these streets, I would go, walk down that street and visit them, taking the same action that I have just described as fool-hardy. Yet, here I'm describing it as an appropriate risk. Why the difference? Simply the intimate connection between the call of God and the action; motivation is central.

Applying this to a fresh expression of church, we are not called to take risks for the sake of being different, showing bravado, enjoying ourselves or upsetting others; this is inappropriate. We take risks when we know that the action is intrinsic to God's call, to the story of which we are a part, not because 'something seems a good idea at the time'.

In his series on cinema music,[11] Neil Brand records how, again and again, producers and directors took risks with the styles and forms of music they used in films; but this was not for the sake of being avant-garde, rather it was to help find the best way to tell the story.

Film composers don't come up with a nice tune or memorable hook. What they do is place their musical abilities at the service of the story . . . They understand about character, narrative and mood and when they bring their music to these elements of cinema they create something that was unimaginable before.

Don't fret, the natural ambience of the church is one of risk-taking, and in the adventure of fresh expressions of church, risks will come; we must pray for the wisdom to discern which are the appropriate ones and for the courage to take them.

Sometimes our challenge is not lack of vision or enthusiasm, or an unwillingness to take risk, but simply weariness; of lack of energy. This is the second theme we alluded to earlier, which we now want to explore. In the Church of Scotland, we've found that many in our church communities are tired, they feel stretched; it seems, in their experience, that too often, too few are doing too much. They can feel misunderstood, imposed upon and unappreciated; another suggestion, no matter how good it may be, will only be a burden, which will leave them feeling guilty, inadequate or discouraged. They really do want to engage in mission, but can't see how they can. This, in our experience, is often profoundly felt by leaders.

Sometimes, the resolution, or part of it, is to evaluate what we are already doing and then act accordingly. We may need to take time to be still and listen for the wisdom of the Spirit. Why are we doing what we are doing? What should cease, what should continue and what should begin? Implementation of the answers may call for great courage.

Another consideration, particularly when we are thinking of developing something new, is to ask ourselves what gives us energy and what drains our energy. We have found this question a very helpful one, when weariness threatens to quell enthusiasm.

Think, for a moment, of your favourite Christmas dinner. You've just had starters and seconds, if not thirds, of the main course and you are full; you feel that you couldn't eat another bite. Then . . . along comes your favourite pudding and suddenly you have 'another stomach'. Why?

Or, imagine it's Friday night and you are at the end of a really hectic week; you are dog-tired and you just want to crash out and watch something undemanding on television, or simply fall asleep on the sofa. You want the world to leave you alone. Then the phone rings; you toy with not answering it . . . but you do. Now imagine two different scenarios. The first is that the caller is someone whom you don't really know all that well and they want your help. Not only do they want your help, but they need it immediately and not only do they need it immediately, but they need your help with one of the things you like doing least. At that moment, whatever energy you felt you had slips away like sand through your fingers.

Now the second scenario: the caller is one of your best friends and you both share a passion for your local football club.[12] Your friend has just got two, last-minute tickets for tonight's match. As it is the cup semi-final and tickets are like gold-dust, you can hardly believe what you are hearing. Suddenly you have a wave of energy; before you know it, you've put your coat on and you are racing to the football ground to meet your friend. Why? What makes the difference in the two scenarios?

For all of us, there are those things which intrinsically enthuse us and those things which bore us; those things for which we'll nearly always find the energy and those things to which we'll be dragged 'kicking and screaming'; and it has nothing to do with the activity as such, but with us and our preferences. Others will love what we avoid and vice versa; those activities that will make 'watching paint dry' an attractive option say nothing about their worth, or otherwise. We should bear in mind this dynamic when we think about mission.

We will, of course, at times, need to engage with things we don't enjoy, sometimes for much longer than we would like. The awareness of what gives us energy and what drains it is not to help us dodge the difficult, but to help us know where our heart is; for where our heart is, we will more easily find enthusiasm, energy and sustainability. If we feel swamped by the need around us, or stretched almost to breaking point, it may help to look to those groups, which, when we think about them, ignite an enthusiasm and new-found or unexpected energy. In our church community, let's recognise not only abilities and spiritual gifts, but also the interests and hobbies that people pursue and the areas of service in which they are involved. Might these be indicators of where our church community might naturally have the energy to develop and sustain fresh expressions of church?

A fresh expression of church is often 'low maintenance', particularly if it is built upon existing relationships and enthusiasm. It need not demand much finance or even extra time as we intentionally 'be' who we are in those settings to which, for whatever reason, we are attracted or may already be a part of.

One final theme is something to which we have alluded indirectly: the giving of a gift. Giving is at the heart of grace, and grace is at the heart of walking with Jesus. So, by going into a community with the heart to develop a fresh expression of church, we open that community to a gift of grace; in this case, the gift of being a church that expresses, with integrity, the recipients' culture. Giving a gift can be a real celebration of love and generosity, but at times it can mask less noble motives. Even if we do not use gifts to ensure loyalty, or to encourage support or compliance (as did Anglo-Saxon lords), we need to be aware that, in other ways, we too can give gifts in order essentially to serve ourselves rather than others. An adult can give a child a gift, hoping to relive their own childhood or youth through the gift; in practice, they never really allow it to belong to the one who has received it. It is not that guidance might not be helpful, but the recipient should be allowed to use the gift in the way that they choose, not in the way that best pleases the giver. So it is with fresh expressions of church: we must not, even indirectly, control or shape the gift that we are bearing to suit us and our pleasure or comfort.

In drawing to a close this brief look at our experience of fresh expressions of church in Scotland, may we leave with you two thoughts. First, never cease to be open to the embrace of God's deep love for you, as an individual and as a church community: experience this, don't merely speculate and talk about it. And from this love, love others, so that they might know God's love for them and how precious they are; so that they might know life through Jesus.

Second, an old Spanish phrase: 'Vaya con Dios'. Unlike the word 'Goodbye', which originates from the phrase 'God be with you', the phrase 'Vaya con Dios' means 'May you go with

PEARL LAVERS
1919 – 2003

Psalm 40:9 (New Living Bible)

I have told all your people about your faithfulness. I have not been afraid to speak out, as you alone, O Lord well know; I have not kept this goodness hidden in my heart.

'What is dying?'

What is dying?   A ship sails and I stand watching till she fades on the horizon, and someone at my side says, "She's gone".

Gone where? Gone from my sight, that's all; she is just as large as when I saw her......the diminished size and total loss of sight is in me, not in her. And just at the moment when someone at my side says, "She's gone", there are others who are watching her coming, and other voices take up a glad shout, "Here she comes!"........ and that is dying.

Bishop Brent

2nd December 2003

God'; there is a world of difference in the two. We end our time together hoping not that we will ask God to go to those places of our choosing, but that we will go with God; to those places where he calls us in the adventure of fresh expressions of church.

Vaya con Dios.

Notes

1 Curtis, Adam, 'HyperNormalisation' (BBC iPlayer, 2016). 'Our world is strange and often fake and corrupt. But we think it's normal because we can't see anything else. HyperNormalisation – the story of how we got here. We live in a time of great uncertainty and confusion. Events keep happening that seem inexplicable and out of control. Donald Trump, Brexit, the war in Syria, the endless migrant crisis, random bomb attacks. And those who are supposed to be in power are paralysed – they have no idea what to do. This film is the epic story of how we got to this strange place. It explains not only why these chaotic events are happening – but also why we, and our politicians, cannot understand them. It shows that what has happened is that all of us in the West – not just the politicians and the journalists and the experts, but we ourselves – have retreated into a simplified and often completely fake version of the world. But because it is all around us we accept it as normal. But there is another world outside. Forces that politicians tried to forget and bury forty years ago – that then festered and mutated – but which are now turning on us with a vengeful fury. Piercing though the wall of our fake world.' From BBC iPlayer website. (Available online at www.bbc.co.uk/programmes/p04b183c).

2 Harari, Yuval Noah, *Sapiens: A Brief History of Humankind* (London: Vintage, 2011).

3 Scharmer, Otto and Kaufer, Katrin, *Leading from the Emerging Future: From Ego-System to Eco-System Economies* (San Francisco: Berret-Koehler Publications, 2013).

4 For an explanation of Theory U, see Scharmer, Otto, *Theory U: Leading from the Future as It Emerges – The Social Technology of Presencing* (San Francisco: Berret-Koehler Publications, 2009).

5 Scharmer and Kaufer, *Leading from the Emerging Future*, p. 21.

6 www.afternow.co.uk.

7 On the AfterNow website, the evidence is presented for this as well as considering some of the implications for society.

8 Love entails the risk of rejection, and God created us as beings who could love him, others and creation.

9 This was at a Fresh Expressions Partnership Hub in 2015.

10 2 Kings 19:14–19.

11 *Sound of Cinema: Music that made the Movies*, episode 3. BBC, 26 September 2013.

12 Read in here whatever is your favourite hobby or interest and apply.

Appendices

Appendix 1

The Eight Fresh Expressions of Church Which Were Interviewed

1 *Gateways*, in the village of Paxton on the Scottish Borders – Rural.
2 *Hot Chocolate*, in the city of Dundee – Urban, city centre.
3 *Neither Young Nor Old* (NYNO), in the city of Aberdeen – Urban, 1940s' housing scheme.
4 *Netherlorn Churches*, in Argyll – Rural and Island rural.
5 *Sanctuary First*, internet and social media based – International: Cyberspace, with face-to-face options.
6 *St George's Tron*, in the city of Glasgow – Urban, city centre.
7 *St Kentigern's*, in the town of Kilmarnock – Urban, 1960s' housing scheme.
8 *The Shed*, in the port of Stornoway – Urban, in a largely rural island context (Lewis).

Appendix 2
Contributors

Siân Ashby

Siân Ashby was born in Northern Ireland, but grew up on the south coast of Spain. She moved to Scotland in 2003 to attend the University of Glasgow where she studied physiology and, later, public health. She spent nine years working in a variety of contexts including the NHS and voluntary sector.

In 2016 she moved to England and now lives with her husband near Peterborough. She is currently working with 'Hope into Action', an organisation that works in partnership with local churches to provide homes for the most vulnerable in society.

Albert Bogle

Albert Bogle is a former Moderator of the General Assembly of the Church of Scotland. He studied theology at both Glasgow and Edinburgh Universities. He was parish minister for thirty-four years leading a multidisciplinary team working to effect transformation in communities at a local national and international level.

He is founder of the Vine Trust, an international volunteering organisation working in the Amazon and Lake Victoria. Albert's ministry has included blogging, broadcasting and developing digital media as a communication tool. In April 2016, he was appointed leader of Sanctuary First, an Online

Worshipping Community exploring new ways to connect and re-engage the faith of those disconnected from church.

Andrea Boyes

Andrea Boyes is a wife, mum of three and a Church of Scotland minister. Andrea began her ministry in a priority area church in Larkhall and was there for several years before a call to the rural parish of Durness and Kinlochbervie. She has a heart for mission, discipleship and church planting and presently serves on the Mission and Discipleship Council of the Church of Scotland.

Helen Brough

Helen Brough is the Director of Forge Scotland – a training and resourcing organisation for new missional communities and expressions of church.

She is based in Dundee where for the last sixteen years she has been investing incarnationally with women and families on the margins and is now exploring developing new missional communities in the city. She is passionate to see the body of Christ equipped and resourced to engage with the missional opportunities in Scotland.

She is married to Colin, has three sons and loves Dundee, coffee and new adventures!

Liz Crumlish

Liz Crumlish is a Church of Scotland minister who has worked in hospital chaplaincy, parish ministry and now grapples with renewing culture in congregations. Liz lives on the west coast of Scotland and walks with God along the beach in all weathers. Liz is a board member of RevGalBlogPals, an international, online community supporting women in ministry and blogs at http://liz-vicarofdibley.blogspot.com.

Lesley Hamilton-Messer

Lesley Hamilton-Messer, originally from Glasgow, now lives in Edinburgh with her husband, Alan. Moving from engineering to studying religion, then mission and evangelism, Lesley's innate curiosity about how things work and 'why are we doing it that way?' transferred easily into her current role in the Church of Scotland. Working in the Church Without Walls team, which has a remit for mission, renewal and fresh expressions, is a more kindly way of saying she is often a 'professional irritant'!

Michael Harvey

Michael Harvey has spoken to thousands of church leaders in his seminars and has to date seen hundreds of thousands of Christians mobilised to invite others to church services and events. This has resulted in 1 million+ accepted invitations, where many 'God conversations' have taken place.

He launched the first National Weekend of Invitation in June 2018. He is author of the books *Unlocking the Growth* and *Creating a Culture of Invitation* and as an itinerant speaker he has a ministry across eighteen countries and five continents.

David Logue

David Logue grew up on the east coast of Scotland and studied at Edinburgh University. He was married in 1973 and moved to west Argyll in 1979. David embraced Christianity while a student and was influenced by both Francis Schaeffer of L'Abri and the charismatic renewal. David was active in his local Church of Scotland for nearly forty years and, on retiring from paid employment, he and his wife undertook the Forge International Pioneer course on church planting and also attended the Going for Growth summer schools. He is currently assisting the local Church of Scotland in vacancy and leading a home group following on from several Alpha groups.

David McCarthy

Born in rural Northern Ireland, David McCarthy has worked with inherited expressions of church in Belfast and in pioneering fresh expressions of church in Andalucia, Spain and in Greenock, Scotland.

He has also worked with parachurch groups: with students in the north of England and in cross-denominational work in Northern Ireland.

Since 2014 he has been the Church of Scotland Fresh Expressions Development Worker.

Tommy MacNeil

Tommy MacNeil has been minister of Martin's Memorial, Stornoway for the last twelve years. During this time, they have witnessed significant growth and development as a church and in their community, especially through The Shed Project. He is convenor of the Recruitment Task Group within Ministries Council and is a part-time lecturer with Highland Theological College where he teaches on evangelism. He is married to Donna and they have two adult children, Joanne (and husband Ali) and Matthew.

Angus Mathieson

Angus Mathieson is Secretary to the Church of Scotland's Mission and Discipleship Council. He was previously with the

Church's Ministries Council and was involved with overseeing strategic deployment of ministries, as well as Fresh Expressions and Emerging Church, to name but two of his responsibilities.

Angus was ordained in 1988 and then spent nine years living in a housing scheme in Ayr, working as a community minister. He has studied in Glasgow, Edinburgh and Tübingen Universities.

He is passionate about developing people's gifts; exploring how we grow as people seeking to follow Jesus; and joining in with what God is doing in the Church – and in the world.

Peter Neilson

After forty-plus years of ministry within the Church of Scotland in a range of roles from parish ministry in Glasgow and Edinburgh to national roles in mission, Peter Neilson retired in 2013 from his role as a freelance mission consultant. He lives in the fishing village of Anstruther with his wife Dorothy, where he is involved in preaching and teaching in the Presbytery of St Andrews. On the family front, Dorothy and Peter have three married daughters and six grandchildren.

Norman Smith

Originally from Lewis in the Western Isles, Norman Smith states, 'I have always had a passion to see people come to Jesus. This has been an anchor point of faith for me in over twenty years of ministry in both rural and urban congregations and in the wider work of the church.'

Appendix 3
About The Church of Scotland

The church communities interviewed in this book are mainly from a Church of Scotland context.

The following brief notes from the church's website help give a sense of the church and its understanding of itself: www. churchofscotland.org.uk.

> The Church of Scotland seeks to inspire the people of Scotland and beyond with the Good News of Jesus Christ through enthusiastic worshipping, witnessing, nurturing and serving communities.
>
> The Church of Scotland is one of the largest organisations in the country. We have over 340,000 members, with more regularly involved in local congregations and our work. Within the organisation, we have around 800 ministers serving in parishes and chaplaincies, supported by more than 1500 professional and administrative staff. Most of our parishes are in Scotland, but there are also churches in England, Europe and overseas.
>
> The Church of Scotland works with communities worldwide . . . [it] has a pivotal role in Scottish society and indeed religion throughout the world.

How We Are Organised

The Church of Scotland's governing system is presbyterian, which means that no one person or group within the Church has more influence or say than any other. The Church does not have one person who acts as the head of faith, as that role is the Lord God's. Its supreme rule of faith and life is through the teachings of the Bible.

Articles Declaratory of the Constitution of the Church of Scotland

The articles declaratory of the Church's constitution lay out our structure, how we govern and membership details . . .

. . . Act Declaratory III: This Church is in historical continuity with the Church of Scotland which was reformed in 1560, whose liberties were ratified in 1592, and for whose security provision was made in the Treaty of Union of 1707. The continuity and identity of the Church of Scotland are not prejudiced by the adoption of these Articles. As a national Church representative of the Christian Faith of the Scottish people it acknowledges its distinctive call and duty to bring the ordinances of religion to the people in every parish of Scotland through a territorial ministry.

Government

Church of Scotland government is organised on the basis of courts, mainly along lines set between 1560 and 1690. Each of these courts has committees, which may include other members of the Church, and at national level employ full-time staff.

At a local level, the parish, the court is a kirk session. Kirk sessions oversee the local congregation and its parish, and consist of elders presided over by a minister.

At district level, the court is a presbytery. Presbyteries consist of all the ministers in the district and an equal number of elders, along with members of the diaconate (a form of ordained ministry, usually working in a complementary role in a ministry team in both parish and industry sector contexts).

There are forty-six presbyteries across Scotland, England, Europe and Jerusalem.

At national level, the court is the highest court of the Kirk, the General Assembly. The General Assembly consists of around 400 ministers, 400 elders, and members of the diaconate, all representing the presbyteries.

Council of Assembly

At the 2019 General Assembly of the Church of Scotland the decision was taken to replace the Council of Assembly with a new Trustee Body, which has the authority to take administrative decisions between General Assemblies, co-ordinate the work of the Church's central administration and take decisions about resources, finances and staffing. Significant changes were also made to its Council and Presbytery structures.

General Trustees

The Church of Scotland General Trustees form a statutory corporation set up in 1921 to hold properties and investments for the Church as a whole.

Some Resources to Help You Continue Exploring . . .

There are many books, videos, websites and other resources to help us explore the world of fresh expressions of church; below is merely a short 'starter'.

Groups

- Fresh Expressions Networks Ltd: http://freshexpressions. org.uk.
- fx resourcing Ltd: www.fxresourcing.org.
- Church Mission Society: https://churchmissionsociety.org/.
- Messy Church: www.messychurch.org.uk/.
- Forge Scotland: http://forgescotland.com/.
- The World Council of Churches documentation and discussion around the Together Towards Life document and the follow-up Arusha documentation, conference and discussion on discipleship: www.oikoumene.org/en/.
- The 'Talking Jesus' research and follow-up material: https://talkingjesus.org/research/.

Books

Aisthorpe, Steve, *The Invisible Church* (Edinburgh: Saint Andrew Press, 2016). A deeply pastoral, mission-focused and accessible book, based on the author's doctoral thesis, which looks at what we can learn from the experiences of 'churchless' Christians. Informed by reflection on Scripture, it paints a picture which is less about decline and more about transition.

Fresh Expression (UK) SHARE series of booklets on beginning and sustaining a fresh expression of church.

Lings, George, *Reproducing Church* (Abingdon: The Bible Reading Fellowship, 2017). A deeply thoughtful and practical book on fresh expressions of church, based on over two decades of experience, reflection and extensive research.

Male, Dave, *How to Pioneer: even if you haven't a clue* (London: Church House Publishing, 2016). 'Brilliant in its simplicity . . . an easy-to-read, practical guide . . . it has the wonderful sense when you read it of making you think, "I can do this", which is the point – you can.' Jonny Baker.

Moynagh, Michael and Philip Harrold, *Church for Every Context* (London: SCM Press, 2012) and *Church in Life* (London: SCM Press, 2017). These two books consider the theology, theory and practice of fresh expressions of church in great depth.

Moynagh, Michael and Rob Peabody, *Refresh* (Oxford: Monarch Books, 2016). A thirty-minute read 'guerrilla manual' on fresh expressions of church.

Moynagh, Michael, *Being Church and Doing Life* (Oxford: Monarch Books, 2014). An accessible, earthed in practice look at the theology and the development of fresh expressions of church. Full of examples and practical wisdom.

Potter, Phil, *Pioneering a New Future: A guide to shaping change and changing the shape of church* (Abingdon: The Bible Reading Fellowship, 2015). Based on the author's wide experience, this book looks first at the practicalities of shaping change of any sort within a church community context and then highlights the need to change the shape of church, with a particular focus on fresh expressions of church.

Bibliography

Aisthorpe, Steve, *The Invisible Church* (Edinburgh: St Andrew Press, 2016).

Bevans, Stephen B. and Schroeder, Roger P., *Constants in Context: A Theology for Mission Today* (Maryknoll, NY: Orbis, 2004).

Bosch, David J., *A Spirituality of the Road* (Scottdale, PA: Herald Press, 1979).

Bridges, William, *Managing Transition: Making the Most of Change* (Cambridge, MA: Da Capo Press, 2003).

Buchan, John, *Mr Standfast* (1919), in *The Complete Richard Hannay Stories* (Ware: Wordsworth Classics, 2010).

Cole, Neil, *Organic Church: Growing Faith Where Life Happens*, 1st edn (San Francisco, CA: Jossey-Bass, 2005).

Cray, Graham (ed.), *Mission-Shaped Church* (Norwich: Church House Publishing, 2004).

Dante, *Divine Comedy*, trans. Allen Mandelbaum (London: Everyman's Library, 1995).

Dalrymple, Theodore, *Our Culture, What's Left of It: The Mandarins and the Masses* (Chicago: Ivan R. Dee, 2005).

Defoe, Daniel, *Robinson Crusoe* (1719).

Donovan, Vincent J., *Christianity Rediscovered* (Maryknoll, NY: Orbis Books, 1978).

Forrest, Carter, *The Rebel Outlaw: Josey Wales* (Whipporwill Publishers, 1972) republished in 1975 under the title *Gone to Texas*.

Gaita, R., *Common Humanity: Thinking About Love and Truth and Justice* (Melbourne: Routledge, 1999).

Grundy, Malcolm, *Multi-Congregational Ministry: Theology and Practice for a Changing Church* (Norwich: Canterbury Press, 2015).

Harari, Yuval Noah, *Sapiens: A Brief History of Humankind* (London: Vintage, 2011).

Hirsch, A, *Forgotten Ways* (Ada, MI: Brazos Press, 2016).

Küng, Hans, *The Church* (London: Burns and Oates, 1968).

Lawrence, Colonel Thomas Edward, *Seven Pillars of Wisdom* (Ware: Wordsworth Editions, 1997 [1927]).

Lewis, C. S., *The Complete Chronicles of Narnia* (London: Collins, 1998).

Lewis, C. S., 'The Last Battle', in *The Complete Chronicles of Narnia* (London: Collins, 1998).

Lewis, C. S., 'The Lion, the Witch and the Wardrobe', in *The Complete Chronicles of Narnia* (London: Collins, 1998).

Lings, George, *Reproducing Churches* (Abingdon: Bible Reading Fellowship, 2017).

Male, Dave, *How to Pioneer: Even if you haven't a clue* (London: Church House Publishing, 2016).

Moynagh, Michael, *Being Church and Doing Life* (Oxford: Monarch Books, 2014).

Moynagh, Michael and Harrold, Philip, *Church for Every Context* (London: SCM Press, 2012).

Moynagh, Michael, *Church in Life* (London: SCM Press, 2017).

Moynagh, Michael and Peabody, Rob, *Refresh* (Oxford: Monarch Books, 2016).

Obermiller, Philip J., Wagner, Thomas E. and Tucker, E. Bruce, *Appalachian Odyssey: Historical Perspectives on the Great Migration* (Westport, CT: Praeger, 2000).

Orwell, George, *Animal Farm* (London: Secker and Warburg, 1945).

Potter, Phil, *Pioneering a New Future: A guide to shaping change and changing the shape of church* (Abingdon: The Bible Reading Fellowship, 2015).

Roberts, David, *Shipwrecked on the Top of the World: Four Against the Arctic* (London: Simon and Schuster, 2003).

Rorty, Amélie (ed.), *Philosophers in Education: Historical Perspectives* (London: Routledge, 1998).

Ross, Kenneth R., Keum, Jooseop, Avtzi, Kyriaki and Hewitt, Roderick R. (eds), *Ecumenical Missiology: Changing Landscapes and New Conceptions of Mission* (Oxford: Regnum / Geneva: World Council of Churches 2016).

Sartre, Jean-Paul, *Nausea* (Harmondsworth: Penguin, 1976 [1938]).

Scharmer, Otto, *Theory U: Leading from the Future as It Emerges – The Social Technology of Presencing* (San Francisco: Berret-Koehler Publications, 2009).

Scharmer, Otto and Kaeufer, Katrin, *Leading from the Emerging Future: From Ego-System to Eco-System Economies* (San Francisco: Berret-Koehler Publications, 2013).

Scott, Cavan and Wright, Mark, *Wit, Wisdom and Timey-Wimey Stuff* (London: BBC Books, 2014).

Singlehurst, Laurence, *Cell Planting: Putting the 'Go' Back into Church* (Cel UK Training Series, 2009).

Sparks, Paul, Soerens, Tim and Friesen, Dwight J., *The New Parish: How Neighborhood Churches Are Transforming Mission, Discipleship and Community* (Downers Grove, IL: Intervarsity Press, 2014).

Stott, John, *The Message of Acts*, BST series (London: Intervarsity Press, 1990).

Tolkien, J. R. R., *The Lord of the Rings* (London: Allen and Unwin, 1954).

Tozer, A. W., *Born After Midnight* (Camp Hill, PA: Christian Publications, 1992 [1959]).

Vance, J. D., *Hillbilly Elegy: A Memoir of a Family and Culture in Crisis* (New York: HarperCollins, 2016).

Wilde Oscar, *The Complete Works of Oscar Wilde* (Glasgow: Geddes and Grosset, 2001).

Williams, Rowan, *Faith in the Public Square* (London: Bloomsbury, 2012).

Williams, Rowan, *The Edge of Words* (London: Bloomsbury, 2014).

Williams, Rowan, *The Lion's World* (London: SPCK, 2012).

Wright, Tom, *Acts for Everyone* (London: SPCK, 2008).
Wright, Tom, *Simply Good News* (London: SPCK, 2015).
Wright, Tom, *Surprised by Hope* (London: SPCK, 2007).
Wright, Tom, *The Day the Revolution Began* (London: SPCK, 2016).
Wyss, Johann, *The Swiss Family Robinson* (1812).

Note on Bible Translations

Scripture quotations are taken from the following versions of the Bible.

Good News Translation (GNT), published by The Bible Societies/HarperCollins Publishers Ltd UK © American Bible Society, 1966, 1971, 1976, 1992. Used by permission.

King James Version (KJV), the rights in which are vested in the Crown, are reproduced by permission of the Crown's Patentee, Cambridge University Press.

New American Standard Bible (NASB) © 1960, 1962, 1963, 1968, 1971, 1972, 1973, 1975, 1977, 1995 by The Lockman Foundation. Used by permission. www.lockman.org.

New International Bible (NIV) © 1973, 1978, 1984 by Biblica (formerly International Bible Society). Used by permission of Hodder & Stoughton Ltd, a member of the Hodder Headline Ltd.

New Living Translation (NLT) © 1971. Used by permission of Tyndale House Publishers, Inc., Carol Stream, Illinois 60188. All rights reserved.

The Passion Translation (TPT) © 2017, 2018 by Passion & Fire Ministries, Inc. Used by permission. All rights reserved. www.ThePassionTranslation.com.

Index of Bible References

Index of Names and Subjects